DIGITAL PHOTO PROJECTS

NICK VANDOME

In easy steps is an imprint of Computer Step
Southfield Road . Southam
Warwickshire CV47 0FB . United Kingdom
www.ineasysteps.com

Notice of Liability
Every effort has been made to ensure that this book contains
accurate and current information. However, Computer Step and the
author shall not be liable for any loss or damage suffered by readers
as a result of any information contained herein.

Trademarks
All trademarks are acknowledged as belonging to their respective
companies.

Photo Credits
Photographs by Euan Turner: pages 13, 28, 36, 42, 67, 73 (middle),
77, 80, 94, 97, 144, 149, 150 (top), 151 (top), 158, 172 and 178. All
other images by Nick Vandome.

Printed and bound in the United Kingdom

ISBN 1-84078-268-4

Contents

Image editing tools

This chapter gives an overview of the most commonly used digital image editing tools. It shows how to use them and this information can be used to complete the projects in the rest of the book.

Covers

Chapter One

About this book

The world of digital photography has advanced considerably since it first broke into the consumer market. When the first digital cameras were available, users were delighted just to see their images appear on a computer screen. However, users have now developed a considerable sophistication and want to be able to create an increasing range of effects with their digital images.

This book seeks to expand your knowledge of digital images by showing you the techniques and tools that can be used to create a variety of projects. This chapter details the standard image editing tools that can be used to manipulate and enhance images. The rest of the book contains step-by-step projects that are fun to do and enable you to become familiar with a variety of image editing techniques.

The techniques used in creating the projects in this book can also be used to create more projects of your own. Once you have mastered these techniques you can let your creative talents go wild.

The projects in this book can be created with most image editing programs. However, for the sake of consistency, the bestselling program, Adobe Photoshop Elements, has been used to create the projects (this is virtually the same as the industry-standard professional package Adobe Photoshop). In addition, the necessary steps are also included for two other popular image editing programs: Paint Shop Pro and PhotoImpact.

Even if you do not own a digital camera it is still possible to complete the projects in this book. All the images used are available to download from the publisher's website at http://www.ineasysteps.com/books/?1840782684 or http://www.ineasysteps.com/books/downloads. Once you have downloaded the images you can work through the projects exactly as they are in the book.

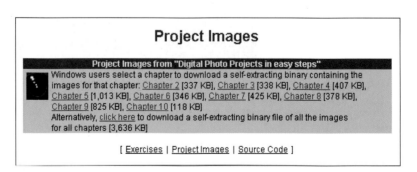

Project Images

Project Images from "Digital Photo Projects in easy steps"

Windows users select a chapter to download a self-extracting binary containing the images for that chapter: Chapter 2 [337 KB], Chapter 3 [338 KB], Chapter 4 [407 KB], Chapter 5 [1,013 KB], Chapter 6 [346 KB], Chapter 7 [425 KB], Chapter 8 [378 KB], Chapter 9 [825 KB], Chapter 10 [118 KB]
Alternatively, click here to download a self-extracting binary file of all the images for all chapters [3,636 KB]

[Exercises | Project Images | Source Code]

The programs

Photoshop Elements

Photoshop Elements is produced by Adobe, the market leader in image editing software. Elements is a consumer level version of the industry standard Photoshop program. Elements contains most of the power of Photoshop, except for the high-end functions required for professional printing. In addition, it also contains enough useful Help features to make the learning curve a smooth one.

Further details about Photoshop Elements can be found on the Adobe website at: http://www.adobe.com/products/photoshopel/main.html

The Photoshop Elements interface contains all of the items that are required to produce a variety of digital imaging projects:

If any tools in the Toolbox have a small arrow in the bottom right corner it means there are additional, related tools that can be accessed. To do this, click and hold on the arrow and select a tool from the menu that appears.

Menu bar   Shortcuts bar   Options bar   Palette well

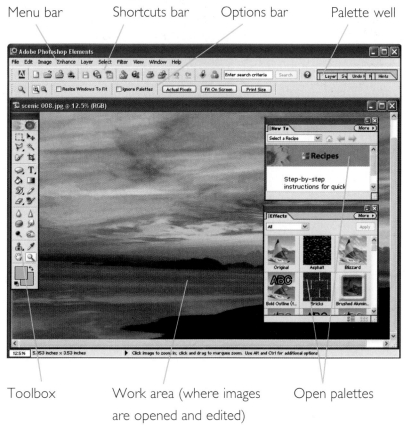

Toolbox   Work area (where images   Open palettes
                 are opened and edited)

Paint Shop Pro

Paint Shop Pro is produced by JASC and is another popular image editing program that has a wide range of functions for editing images and creating graphics. Throughout the book, the relevant Paint Shop Pro commands will be included in tips in the margin if they are substantially different from the Photoshop Elements ones. For more information about Paint Shop Pro, look at the JASC website at www.jasc.com

Menu bar　　　　　　　　　　　　　　　　　Toolbars

Tools toolbar

Work area (where images are opened and edited)

Open palettes

PhotoImpact

PhotoImpact is produced by Ulead and is similar in terms of power and functionality to Photoshop Elements and Paint Shop Pro. As with Paint Shop Pro, the commands that are relevant to PhotoImpact will also be included in tips in the margin. For more information about PhotoImpact, look at the Ulead website at www.ulead.com

Menu bar   Toolbars

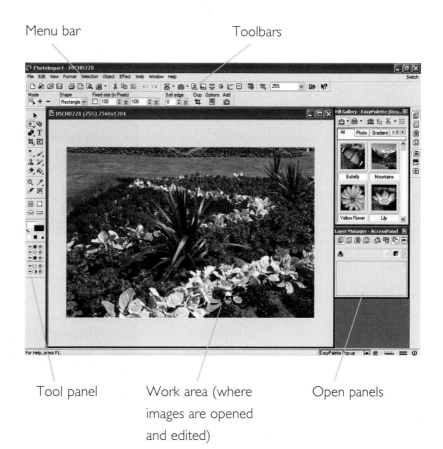

Tool panel   Work area (where   Open panels
                    images are opened
                    and edited)

Move tool

Selecting and moving items within digital images is a fundamental part of image editing. This is particularly important when dealing with some of the more intricate operations that occur with varied digital photo projects. The Move tool can be used to move parts of an image once they have been selected with one of the selection tools (for details of selecting areas, see pages 15–17). To use the Move tool:

In Paint Shop Pro, the Move tool is denoted by a four-headed arrow.

In PhotoImpact, the Move tool is called the Pick tool.

1 Select an area within an image

2 Click once on the Move tool to select it

3 Drag the selected area with the Move tool. It can be dragged to a different location in the image

Transforming with the Move tool

In addition to moving selections, the Move tool can also be used to resize and rotate selections. To do this:

 In Paint Shop Pro, use the Deform tool in the Tools toolbar.

Drag here to stretch a selection horizontally or vertically

 In PhotoImpact, use the Transform tool in the Tool panel.

 Hold down Shift and drag the corner resizing handle to resize a selection in proportion.

Drag here to stretch a selection horizontally and vertically

 To rotate a selection, drag just outside the middle resizing handle, rather than directly on it.

Drag here to rotate a selection

Crop tool

Very few images are perfect without any form of editing, even those taken by professional photographers. One of the most common, and effective, editing techniques is cropping. This is where part of the background of an image is removed to give greater prominence to the main subject of the image. This works best when the background is too expansive or distracting. To use the Crop tool:

1 Click once on the Crop tool to select it

2 Drag on an image to select the area you want to keep

Crop selections can also be committed by clicking on the tick button on the Options bar.

3 Press Enter to commit the crop operation

Selection tools

Digital images are made up of tiny colored dots (pixels) that can be considered as the foundations of the images. This makes it possible to select individual parts of an image (from one pixel up to the whole image). Making selections is a vital part of digital image editing as it enables editing techniques to be applied to a part of the image, while the rest remains untouched. There are a number of ways in which areas of an image can be selected:

Rectangular Marquee selection tool

This can be used to make symmetrical, rectangular, selections:

1 Click once on the Rectangular Marquee selection tool to select it

Marquee selection tools are usually grouped together in image editing programs.

2 Drag on an image to make a rectangular selection

Elliptical Marquee selection tool

This is similar to the Rectangular Marquee selection tool, except it is used to make elliptical selections:

1 Click once on the Elliptical Marquee selection tool to select it

2 Drag on an image to make an elliptical selection

Lasso tool

There are three types of lasso tools that can be used to make asymmetrical selections. The simplest is the Lasso tool:

1 Click once on the Lasso tool to select it

2 Drag on an image to make a freehand selection. Return to the starting point to complete the selection

The third type of lasso selection tool is the Magnetic Lasso tool. This works by making an automatic selection as you drag the cursor around an image. The selection is made by identifying areas of contrast in the image and locking to the border between the two colors. Return to the starting point to complete the selection.

Polygonal Lasso tool

This works by placing different selection points around an image:

1 Click once on the Polygonal Lasso tool to select it

2 Click on an image to add a selection point. Move to the next point and click to add additional selection points. Return to the starting point to complete the selection

Magic Wand tool

This is used to select areas of similar color. To do this:

1   Click once on the Magic Wand tool to select it

2   Click on an area
of color to select
it and any
associated areas
of the same, or
similar, color

 *When using the
Magic Wand tool,
there is an option
for setting the
Tolerance in the
Options bar. This determines the
range of color which will be
selected in relation to the initial
color that is selected in an
image.*

3   Hold down
Shift and click
on another
area to add it
to the existing
selection

 *Hold down Alt
and click on a
selection to
deselect it. This
can be useful if
more than one area has been
selected.*

4   Check off the Contiguous box in the
Options bar to allow the selection of similar
colors throughout an image, not just those
that are adjacent to the initial selection

Coloring tools

Coloring tools can be used to change the color of an area within an image or a selection. Coloring tools can be loaded with different colors, as required. To do this:

In Paint Shop Pro, colors can be selected and mixed in the Materials palette which can be accessed by selecting View>Palettes> Materials from the Menu bar.

Click here on the Tools palette to edit the foreground color

Select a color and click OK

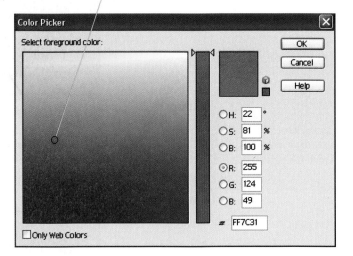

The selected foreground color is used for all coloring tools until a different one is selected

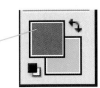

The background color can also be selected in the same way as the foreground color. The background color appears behind items that have been removed or moved in an image

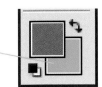

Paint Bucket tool

The Paint Bucket tool can be used to fill in areas with solid color:

In Paint Shop Pro, the Paint Bucket tool is known as the Flood Fill tool.

1 Click here to select the Paint Bucket tool

2 Click on an area of an image or a selection

Pencil tool

The Pencil tool can be used to draw colored lines on images:

By selecting different colors, the Pencil tool can be used to create a fireworks effect on an image.

1 Click here to select the Pencil tool

2 Drag to add colored lines to an image

Text tool

Text can be added to images, to give them an extra dimension. To do this:

1 Click here to select the Text tool

2 Click on an image and start typing to add text

In Paint Shop Pro, text can be formatted using the Tool Options palette, which can be accessed by selecting View>Palettes>Tool Options from the Menu bar.

In PhotoImpact, text can be formatted using the Attribute Toolbar, which can be accessed by selecting View>Toolbars & Panels> Attribute Toolbar from the Menu bar.

3 Select the formatting options, as required, for the text, from the Options bar

Clone tool

The Clone tool provides the facility for copying one area of an image over another. This can be used to remove small blemishes, such as spots and wrinkles, and also larger objects. It can also be used to duplicate elements of an image. To use the Clone tool:

In Paint Shop Pro, the Clone tool is known as the Clone Brush tool. This is loaded by holding down Shift and right clicking.

In PhotoImpact, the Clone tool is known as the Clone-Paintbrush tool. This can be loaded by holding down Shift and left clicking.

1 Click here to select the Clone tool

2 Hold down the Alt key and click on an image to load the Clone tool

3 Drag over the image. The area under the cross is copied wherever the cursor is dragged

Eraser tool

The Eraser tool is used to remove areas of an image. To do this:

1 Click here to select the Eraser tool

2 Drag on an image to remove a part of it. If it is the background image, the background color in the Tools panel will replace the erased area

3 For precise erasing, select an area and then erase within it. The Eraser tool will only be applied within the selection

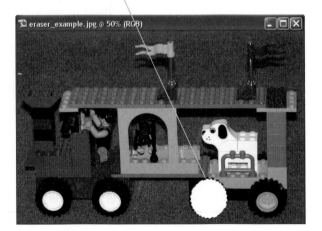

Zoom tool

When working with digital images it is essential to be able to zoom in and out on particular sections of an image. Zooming in allows for very exact editing operations while zooming out enables you to see how editing changes have affected the whole image. To use the Zoom tool:

1 Click here to select the Zoom tool

2 Click on an image to zoom in by incremental amounts

Zooming in on an image is an excellent way to edit individual pixels, such as recoloring eyes that are suffering from red-eye.

3 Drag on an image to zoom in on the selected area

4 Hold down Alt and click on an image to zoom out

Color correction

There are a number of ways in which the color in an image can be improved:

Levels

1. Select Enhance>Adjust Brightness/Contrast>Levels from the Menu bar

In Paint Shop Pro, the color correction commands can be found under the Adjust category on the Menu bar.

2. Drag these sliders to change the color distribution in an image between its darkest and lightest points

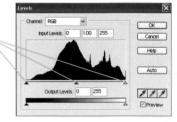

Brightness and Contrast

In PhotoImpact, the color correction commands can be found under the Format category on the Menu bar.

1. Select Enhance>Adjust Brightness/Contrast>Brightness/Contrast from the Menu bar

2. Drag these sliders to change the brightness and contrast of an image or selection

Hue and Saturation

1. Select Enhance>Adjust Color>Hue/Saturation from the Menu bar

2. Drag these sliders to change the hue and saturation of an image or selection

Resizing issues

The issue of resizing images can be a complex one, but for the purpose of these projects the important aspects are resizing the onscreen size of an image and also resizing the canvas on which an image is displayed.

Resizing an image

Check on the Constrain Proportions box to ensure that items are resized proportionally i.e. if one dimension is edited the other one is updated automatically.

1   Select Image>Resize>Image Size from the Menu bar

In Paint Shop Pro, the resizing commands can be found under the Image category on the Menu bar.

2   Check on the Resample Box and enter a new value in the Width or Height boxes. Click OK

In PhotoImpact, the resizing commands can be found under the Format category on the Menu bar.

Resizing the canvas

1   Select Image>Resize>Canvas Size from the Menu bar

2   Enter a new value in the Width or Height boxes. Click OK

Working with layers

When creating digital photo projects, new elements will inevitably be added to the original image. To make it easier to work with different elements within the same image, layers can be used to store separate items:

Although different elements make up a whole image, they can still be edited independently on their own layers

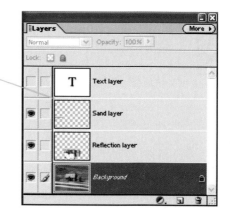

If you are working with more than one item in an image it is usually a good idea to put the different elements on different layers. This makes it easier to work with and edit the image.

Layers palette

The Layers palette can be used to add new layers, select layers within an image, arrange layers and hide and lock layers during editing:

Click here to set a blend mode for two layers

Click here to set a layer's transparency

Click here to lock all layers

When editing items in a layered image, make sure the correct layer is selected for the item you want to edit.

Click here to select a layer (this is the one that can currently be edited in the image)

Click here to hide or reveal a layer

Click here to add a new layer

Click here to delete a layer

Color projects

Color is an essential part of a digital image, but you do not have to stick with the colors that are in the original. This chapter shows how color can be used to create projects that are striking and artistic.

Covers

Chapter Two

It's all in the eyes

A lot of digital image editing programs have a facility for quickly removing red-eye from an image. However, with a bit of imagination it is possible to be a bit more creative with the appearance of someone's eyes. This can include creating colored contact lenses or multi-colored glasses. To do this:

1 Open a suitable image

In Paint Shop Pro, select View> Zoom from the Menu bar. Then use the Preset Shape tool, the Flood Fill tool and the Pen tool.

2 Select the Zoom tool

In PhotoImpact use the Path Drawing tool in the Tool panel.

3 Drag around the eye area to magnify it

4 Select the Ellipse drawing tool

Select the required color for the drawing tool once it has been selected.

5 Draw an ellipse around the eye (for glasses) or the eyeball (for contact lenses). The object is placed on a new layer in the Layers palette

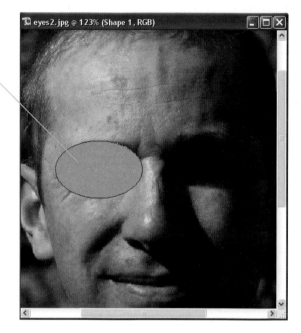

6 Open the Layers palette and click here to select an opacity setting for the selection. Drag on the sliding scale to set the opacity

The opacity of a selection affects how transparent it appears. This is usually set in the Layers palette.

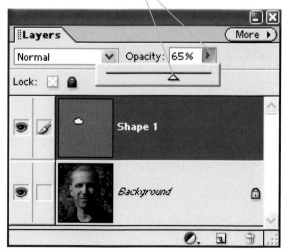

In Paint Shop Pro and PhotoImpact use the Copy and Paste commands to copy the ellipse shape onto a new layer.

7 Select the ellipse and select Layer>Duplicate Layer from the Menu bar

8 Position the new ellipse as required

In Paint Shop Pro, select Layers> Merge>Merge All (Flatten) from the Menu bar to merge the different layers. In PhotoImpact, select Object> Merge All from the Menu bar.

9 Select Layer>Flatten Image from the Menu bar

10 Select the Pencil tool and an appropriate width

In Paint Shop Pro, use the Paint Brush tool to draw on the image.

11 Drag with the Pencil tool to create the desired effect

Changing the sky color

For a lot of photographs, particularly ones of landscapes, the sky can either make or break the image. Thankfully, image editing software can now save the day by enhancing the sky's natural color, or by creating a new, abstract pattern effect.

Enhancing natural color

(Although this example applies just to the sky, the technique can be applied to whole images, or any other areas of an image.)

 In Paint Shop Pro, there is no Polygonal Lasso tool, so use the Magic Wand tool to make the selection. To change the selection, select Adjust>Brightness and Contrast>Brightness/Contrast from the Menu bar.

1 Select the Polygonal Lasso tool or the Magic Wand tool

2 Select the required area in an image by dragging around it with the Polygonal Lasso tool or by clicking with the Magic Wand tool

 In PhotoImpact use the Lasso tool or the Magic Wand tool. Then select Format> Brightness & Contrast from the Menu bar.

3 Select Enhance>Adjust Brightness/Contrast>Brightness/Contrast from the Menu bar

4 Drag the sliders until the desired effect is achieved in the image. Check on the Preview box

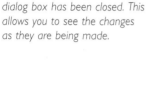

If the Preview box is clicked on, the editing changes will appear in the image before the dialog box has been closed. This allows you to see the changes as they are being made.

Brightness/Contrast

Brightness: `-45`

Contrast: `+24`

OK
Cancel
Help

☑ Preview

5 Click OK

6 The sky color is updated in the image

sky_color2.jpg @ 25% (RGB)

Adding a pattern effect

1 Select the Polygonal Lasso tool or the Magic Wand tool

In Paint Shop Pro, click on the Pattern tab in the Materials palette.

2 Select the required area in an image by dragging around it with the Polygonal Lasso tool or by clicking with the Magic Wand tool

In PhotoImpact, use the Texture Fill tool, which can be accessed from the Bucket Fill tool option on the Tool panel.

3 Select the Pattern Stamp tool

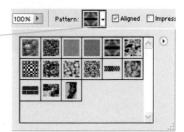

4 Click here to select a pattern style

5 Drag over the selected area to create the pattern effect

Psychedelic effects

Gradient color can be added to areas of an image to give it a psychedelic effect. This can be used effectively for backgrounds, clothes or even buildings. To do this:

1 Select the Polygonal Lasso tool or the Magic Wand tool

2 Select the required area in an image by dragging around it with the Polygonal Lasso tool or by clicking with the Magic Wand tool

In Paint Shop Pro, use the Materials palette to select a gradient and then add it with the Flood Fill tool.

In PhotoImpact gradient colors can be created and selected in the Gradients section of the Color panel.

3 Select the Gradient tool

4 Click here to select the gradient style

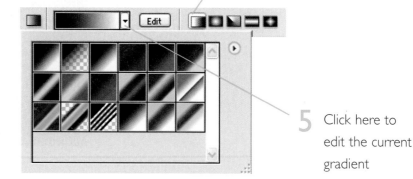

5 Click here to edit the current gradient

6 Click here to select a gradient style

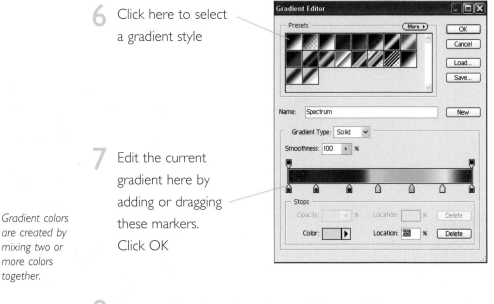

7 Edit the current gradient here by adding or dragging these markers. Click OK

Gradient colors are created by mixing two or more colors together.

8 Drag on the selected area to apply the gradient

Creating abstract posters

One way to make the most of an individual image is to copy it numerous times and apply different color effects to each of the subsequent images. This can be done to great effect by using the image in a poster:

1 Open the image you want to use

In Paint Shop Pro, select Image> Canvas Size from the Menu bar.

In PhotoImpact select Format> Expand Canvas from the Menu bar.

2 Select Image>Resize>Canvas Size from the Menu bar

3 Enter a size for the canvas and click OK

Check the size of the image and increase the size of the canvas proportionally.

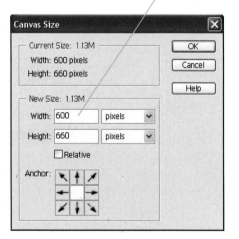

4 Select the Rectangular Marquee tool

5 Select the image on the canvas and select Edit>Cut from the Menu bar

 In PhotoImpact select Edit> Paste>As Object from the Menu bar. The original image will also be visible.

 In Paint Shop Pro, select Edit> Paste>Paste as New Layer from the Menu bar.

6 Select Edit>Paste to add the image back onto the canvas

7 Select the Move tool

8 Drag the image into the required position

 The reason the selection is pasted back into the page is so it can be placed on its own layer, enabling it to be edited independently.

9 Repeat Steps 6–8 for the required number of images

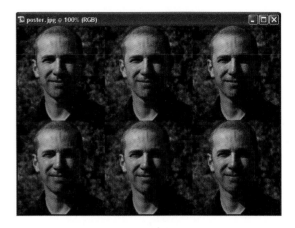

10 Each image is now on a different layer, as shown in the Layers palette

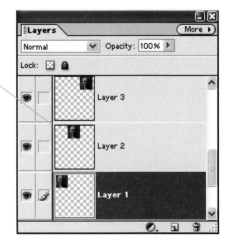

Use the brightness and contrast or the hue and saturation commands to create different effects for each image.

11 Select each image. Apply color effects to each image as required

Use special effect filters to create even more dramatic changes between the images.

Concocting inedible food

There is a very strong connection between the way food looks and our reaction to it. We associate certain foods with particular colors and a fun project is to edit digital images so that the color of the food makes it appear distinctly unappetizing. To do this:

1 Open an appropriate food related image

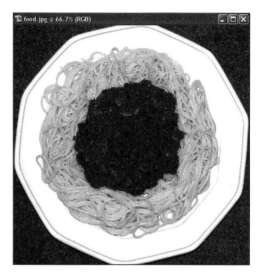

If you are capturing images of hot food, make sure it has cooled down before you take the picture. This will prevent any steam spoiling the final image. If necessary, brush the food with cooking oil to make it glisten more.

2 Select the Polygonal Lasso tool or the Magic Wand tool

3 Select the required food by dragging around it with the Polygonal Lasso tool and clicking where appropriate to add anchor points. Alternatively, click on a color in the image with the Magic Wand tool to select adjacent colors

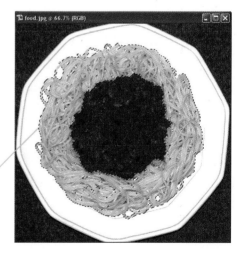

In Paint Shop Pro, select Adjust>Hue and Saturation>Hue/ Saturation/ Lightness from the Menu bar.

4 Select Enhance>Adjust Color>Hue/Saturation from the Menu bar

5 Adjust the hue and saturation as required. Click OK

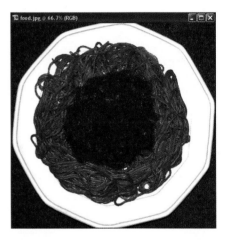

In PhotoImpact select Format> Hue & Saturation from the Menu bar.

6 The effect is applied to the selected area

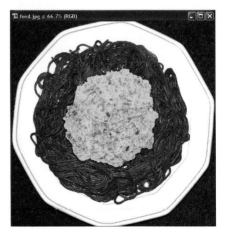

7 Repeat Steps 2–5 as required for the final, unappetizing, effect

Photographic projects

Some images are created as a result of photographic techniques when the picture is captured. This chapter shows how to recreate some of these techniques with image editing software and it also shows how to create photographic effects, such as simulating old photographs or changing the background of an image.

Covers

Chapter Three

Blurring the background

A common photographic technique for giving greater prominence to the main object in an image is to blur the background. This can be done when the image is captured by changing the aperture settings on the camera, and is known as adjusting the depth of field. However, the same effect can be achieved with image editing software. A blurred background can be used for items such as portraits and also for creating the impression of speed for a vehicle or a person. To create a blurred background:

For a project on creating the impression of speed, see Chapter Nine, page 163.

1 Select the Polygonal Lasso tool

In Paint Shop Pro, use the Freehand Selection tool and Selections>Invert from the Menu bar.

2 Select the main object in the image

In PhotoImpact use the Lasso tool or the Magic Wand tool and Selection>Invert from the Menu bar.

3 Select Select>Inverse from the Menu bar to select the background

4 Select Filter>Blur>Gaussian Blur from the Menu bar

 In Paint Shop Pro, select Adjust> Blur>Gaussian Blur from the Menu bar.

5 Enter a value for the amount of blur to be applied. Click OK

 In PhotoImpact select Effect> Blur>Gaussian Blur from the Menu bar.

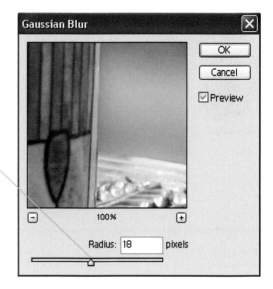

6 The background is blurred accordingly

Repairing old photographs

For anyone with old, faded and torn photographs, an excellent project is to restore them to their former glory. To do this, you have to first scan the image so that you have a digital version with which to work. Once this has been done, some general editing techniques can be applied to repair the image. To do this:

When scanning images, use a high resolution of 600 dpi or above to achieve the highest possible quality.

1 Open the scanned image of the old photograph

In Paint Shop Pro, select Adjust> Brightness and Contrast>Levels from the Menu bar.

2 Select Enhance>Adjust Brightness/Contrast>Levels from the Menu bar

3 Drag the sliders to improve the color in the image. Click OK

In PhotoImpact select Format> Brightness & Contrast from the Menu bar.

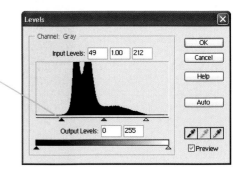

4 Select the Dodge tool and drag it over any areas that need lightening

5 Select the Burn tool and drag it over any areas that need darkening

In Paint Shop Pro, select the Clone Brush tool. This is loaded by holding down Shift and right clicking.

In PhotoImpact select the Clone-Paintbrush and press Shift and left click to load the cloning tool with its starting point.

6 Select the Zoom tool and magnify any areas with creases or tears

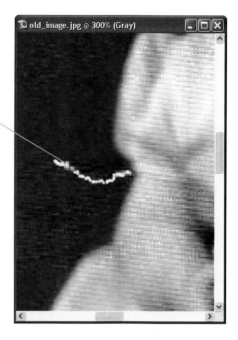

7 Select the Clone tool

8 Hold down Alt and click on the point that you want to use as the starting point for cloning

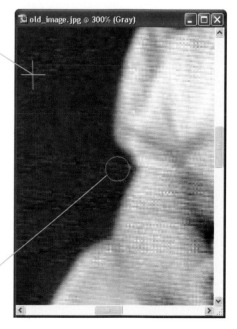

9 Drag the Cloning Stamp tool over the crease or tear

10 Apply color correction techniques e.g. levels and brightness and contrast

11 The image after editing

12 Compare the result in step 11 with the image prior to editing

Creating "new" old photographs

To create an old fashioned effect with digital images it is not necessary to start with an old photograph and scan it into a digital format. It is possible to create this effect, including the brownish sepia effect. To do this:

1 Open an image you want to convert into an old fashioned style

In Paint Shop Pro, select Image> Greyscale from the Menu bar and use the Smudge tool for blurring.

In PhotoImpact select Format> Data Type> Grayscale to create a black and white copy of the original image.

2 Select Enhance> Adjust Color> Remove Color to convert the image to black and white

Set the Blur tool to a low value in the Options bar, otherwise the image will become too blurred.

3 Select the Blur tool and drag it over the image to give it a slightly blurry effect

In Paint Shop Pro, select Adjust> Hue and Saturation>Hue/ Saturation/ Lightness from the Menu bar or select Effects>Sepia Toning from the Menu bar.

4 Select Enhance>Adjust Color>Hue/Saturation from the Menu bar

5 Check on the Colorize box and drag the Hue and Saturation sliders to create the desired effect. Click OK

In PhotoImpact select Format> Hue & Saturation from the Menu bar.

6 The sepia effect is applied to the image

In Paint Shop Pro, select Adjust> Add/Remove Noise>Add Noise from the Menu bar.

In PhotoImpact select Effect> Noise>Add Noise from the Menu bar.

7 Select Filter>Noise>Add Noise from the Menu bar

8 Add a moderate amount of noise by dragging this slider. Click OK

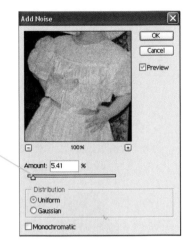

9 Noise gives the image a grainy effect which completes the transformation into a "new" old photograph

Noise is an effect created by randomly distributed colored pixels in an image. Often they are unwanted blemishes, but sometimes noise can be added deliberately to give an image a grainier appearance.

Inserting a new background

Since photography is very rarely an exact science, there are frequently occasions where one part of an image is just as you want it, while the rest is not of the same quality. A common example of this is when the background looks uninspiring or washed-out. To rectify this, the following project can be undertaken to insert a new background from a different image:

1 Open the two images to be combined

In Paint Shop Pro, use the Freehand Selection tool or the Magic Wand tool.

2 Select the Polygonal Lasso tool

3 In the first image, select the area you want to keep as the main object of the image

In PhotoImpact use the Lasso tool or the Magic Wand tool.

4 Select Edit>Copy from the Menu bar

5 Select Edit>Paste from the Menu bar to place the selected area back into the image

In Paint Shop Pro, select Edit> Paste>Paste as New Layer from the Menu bar.

In PhotoImpact select Edit> Paste>As Object from the Menu bar.

6 The selection now appears on its own layer in the Layers palette. Position it exactly in the same position as the background image

7 Access the second image and select the background with the Rectangular Marquee tool

8 Select Edit>Copy from the Menu bar

If you cannot select a particular item in a layered image it is probably because you have the wrong layer selected in the Layers palette.

9 Return to the first image by clicking on it once. Click here on the Layers palette to add a new layer

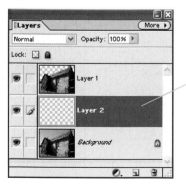

10 Drag the new layer between the two others

11 Select the middle layer and select Edit>Paste to insert the background from the second image. This can be dragged into position with the Move tool, if required

 In Paint Shop Pro, select Edit> Paste>Paste as New Layer from the Menu bar.

 In PhotoImpact select Edit> Paste>As Object from the Menu bar.

12 If required, select the middle layer and adjust the brightness and contrast

13 The final image contains the adjusted background

Being negative

Although digital images do not produce a negative when they are captured, it is possible to recreate a similar effect:

1 Open an image you want to turn into a negative (black and white images give a more accurate negative effect)

In Paint Shop Pro, select Adjust> Negative Image from the Menu bar.

2 Select Image>Adjustments>Invert from the Menu bar

3 The negative effect is displayed

In PhotoImpact select Format> Invert from the Menu bar.

Enlarging an area for printing

Sometimes there will be a part of an image from which you want to obtain a print, while ignoring the rest of the image. This could be achieved by printing out the image and then cutting out the required element. However, this can be unsatisfactory, particularly if the area is relatively small. A better alternative is to crop and enlarge the area that you want to print. To do this:

1   Open an image and, with the Zoom tool selected, zoom in on the area you want to enlarge

2   Select the Crop tool and drag around the desired area. Press Return or Enter to apply the crop

In Paint Shop Pro, select Image> Resize from the Menu bar.

In PhotoImpact select Format> Image Size from the Menu bar.

3   To enlarge the cropped area, select Image> Resize>Image Size from the Menu bar

4   The current size of the cropped area is displayed here

5 Check on the
Constrain Proportions
and Resample Image
boxes and enter a new
value here to enlarge
the image. (The other
dimension is
automatically updated)

6 The image is
enlarged by
adding pixels
to the
existing
image. The
image quality
is slightly
inferior to
the original

*When printing
images at a high
quality, set the
Resolution in the
Document Size
section of the Image Size dialog
box to 150 pixel/inch or above.*

7 In the Image Size
box, the size at
which the image
can be printed can
be altered by
changing the values
in these boxes

Adding and removing projects

Being able to add and remove items in images is one of the most satisfying aspects of digital image editing. This chapter details projects in which the final image is very different from the original, thanks to some inventive editing.

Covers

Chapter Four

Now you see them, now you don't

Cloning can be used to perform a variety of tasks. One of these is to help remove unwanted items from an image. This can include people or buildings and can be done even if the item to be removed is in the center of the image. If this is the case, other items in the image will have to be moved around to cover the gap that is created once the unwanted item has been removed. To do this:

In Paint Shop Pro, use the Freehand Selection tool.

In PhotoImpact use the Lasso tool.

1 Use the Polygonal Lasso tool to select the item to be removed. The selection does not have to be too accurate

2 Delete the selection from the image by selecting Edit> Clear from the Menu bar

Make sure the first selection has been deselected before the second selection is made.

3 Use the Polygonal Lasso tool to select the item to be moved. Again, the selection does not have to be too accurate

4 Select Edit>Cut from the Menu bar to remove the selection

5 In the Layers palette, click here to add a new layer

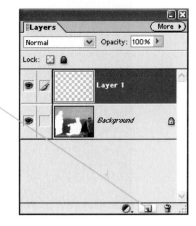

In Paint Shop Pro, select Edit>Paste>Paste as New Layer from the Menu bar.

In PhotoImpact select Edit>Paste>As Object from the Menu bar.

6 Select Edit>Paste from the Menu bar to place the selection on the new layer. Position it as required, using the Move tool

7 Select the Eraser tool and drag to remove any of the selection that is not required. You may want to magnify the selection with the Zoom tool

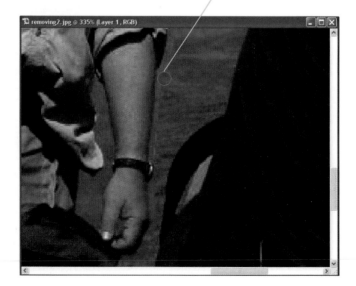

8 Select the original layer and select the Clone tool

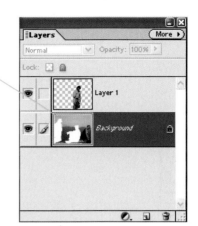

In PhotoImpact use the Clone-Paintbrush tool.

If you do not keep moving the initial cloning point you may end up with a patterned effect rather than a smooth progression.

9 Hold down Alt and click to select the area to use to cover over the holes in the image. Change the cloning point frequently to create a smooth and accurate effect

If you have a white area in an image, as a result of something being deleted, this will be picked up by the Clone tool, unless the initial clone point is moved.

10 Fine-tune the image with any color corrections e.g. brightness and contrast or levels and cropping

Attendance not required

As well as removing people or objects from an image, there are also occasions when it is useful to add them into an image. This is particularly relevant for photographs of groups of people when someone was not available to appear in the original photograph. To do this:

In Paint Shop Pro, use the Freehand Selection tool.

In PhotoImpact use the Lasso tool.

1 Open the group photograph and select the group with the Polygonal Lasso tool. The selection does not have to be too accurate

2 Select Edit>Copy from the Menu bar to copy the selection of the group

3 In the Layers palette, click here to add a new layer

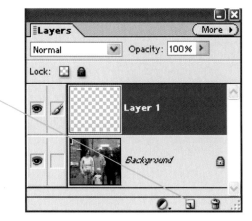

In Paint Shop Pro, select Edit> Paste>Paste as New Layer from the Menu bar, rather than having to create a new layer first.

In PhotoImpact select Edit> Paste>As Object from the Menu bar, rather than having to create a new layer first.

When deleting the edges around the pasted area, click on the eye icon in the Layers palette next to the background layer. This will hide the layer so you get a clearer view of the one above it, on which you will be working.

4   Select Edit>Paste from the Menu bar to place the selection on the new layer. Position it in exactly the same place as the background layer

5   Select the Eraser tool and click and drag to remove any of the selection that is not required. You may want to magnify the selection with the Zoom tool

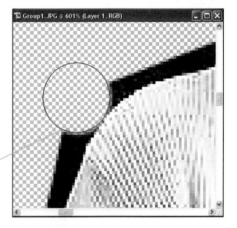

6   Use the Polygonal Lasso tool to select the person who you want to add to the group image. Select Edit>Copy from the Menu bar

...cont'd

7 Create a new layer, in between the two existing layers, and select Edit>Paste from the Menu bar to insert the selection of the individual into the group image

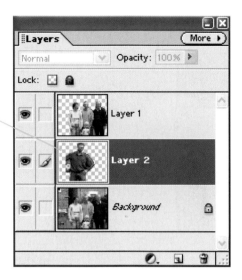

In Paint Shop Pro, select Edit> Paste>Paste as New Layer from the Menu bar.

In PhotoImpact select Edit> Paste>As Object from the Menu bar.

8 The pasted item appears between the background layer and the top layer

9 Select the middle layer, then select Image>Transform>Free Transform from the Menu bar. Drag the resizing handles to resize the individual in proportion with the rest of the image

In Paint Shop Pro, use the Deform tool in the Tools toolbar.

In PhotoImpact, use the Transform tool in the Tool Panel to resize the selection.

10 Complete the image by performing color correction on the middle layer and erasing any unwanted areas around the selection as in Step 5. Finally, crop the whole image, if required

And then there were two

Cloning with an image editing program is the non-controversial way to produce twins, triplets or as many copies of a person or animal as required. To do this:

In Paint Shop Pro, the Clone tool is known as the Clone Brush tool. This is loaded by holding down Shift and right clicking.

In PhotoImpact, the Clone tool is known as the Clone-Paintbrush tool. This can be loaded by holding down Shift and left clicking.

Cloning can also be done between two separate images.

For greater accuracy when cloning an object or person (so you do not get unwanted parts of the background) select it first and use the selection as the area for cloning.

Open an image where there is plenty of space to the side of the main subject

2 Select the Clone tool. Hold down Alt and click on the point where you want to start cloning

3 Drag in the available space to create an identical twin

Performing cosmetic surgery

A potentially perfect photo can sometimes be spoiled by an unwanted spot, wrinkle or blemish appearing on someone's face. However, you can take on the role of cosmetic surgeon and quickly eradicate any unwanted items. (Don't worry about doing this: even models in glossy fashion magazines have usually had some form of digital surgery.) To do this:

In Paint Shop Pro, the Clone tool is known as the Clone Brush tool. This is loaded by holding down Shift and right clicking.

1 Open an image and select the Zoom tool to zoom in on the affected area

In PhotoImpact, the Clone tool is known as the Clone-Paintbrush tool. This can be loaded by holding down Shift and left clicking.

2 Select the Clone tool. Hold down Alt and click on an area of clear skin

3 Drag the Clone tool over the blemish to replace it with the clear skin

Going on an instant diet

If you want to lose a few pounds without the hassle of going on a diet or joining a gym, this is the way to do it:

1 Open an image and select the Zoom tool to zoom in on the affected area

If you are going to use this technique on a friend or a family member, be careful about how you approach the subject!

2 Select the Eraser tool and drag to remove unwanted areas in the image

3 Select the Clone tool to clone the background over the area that has been removed

Special effects projects

This chapter shows you how to get creative with your images and create some trick effects. These include combining different sized images, creating collages, producing animated effects and even creating your own ghosts.

Covers

Chapter Five

Size matters: changing proportions

A project that is always guaranteed to catch people's attention is one where two images have been combined and one of them is resized so that it looks completely out of proportion with the other. This is particularly effective with images of children: they can be placed into unusual situations, such as having a ride on the family pets or other animals. To do this:

1   Capture the two images that are going to be combined. If required, stage the images, keeping in mind how you want the finished project to appear

In Paint Shop Pro, use the Freehand Selection tool.

2   Use the Polygonal Lasso tool to select the object that is going to be resized. Select Edit>Copy from the Menu bar

In PhotoImpact, use the Lasso tool.

In Paint Shop Pro, select Edit> Paste>Paste as New Layer from the Menu bar.

In PhotoImpact, select Edit> Paste>As Object from the Menu bar.

3 Select the second image and select Edit>Paste from the Menu bar to place the selection. It will be placed on a new layer

4 The pasted item appears on its own layer in the Layers palette

5 Select the Zoom tool and zoom in on the pasted item

6 Select the Eraser tool and drag to remove any unwanted parts around the selection

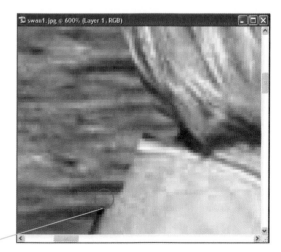

In Paint Shop Pro, use the Deform tool in the Tools toolbar.

In PhotoImpact, use the Transform tool in the Tool panel.

7 Select Image> Transform>Free Transform from the Menu bar and drag the resizing handles as required

8 Select the Move tool and drag the pasted image into the correct position on the background image

9 Use the brightness/ contrast command or the levels command to match the colors of the two images. Crop the final image, if required

Building multi-layered collages

Through the use of layers, complex collages can be created by combining numerous items within a single image. The effect can be made even more dramatic by allowing each layer to interact with the one below it. To do this:

1 Open an image that is going to serve as the background for the collage

2 Open another image and make a selection within it. Select Edit>Copy from the Menu bar

In Paint Shop Pro, select Edit>Paste>Paste as New Layer from the Menu bar.

In PhotoImpact, select Edit>Paste>As Object from the Menu bar.

3 Select the background image and select Edit>Paste from the Menu bar to add the selection. At this point, only the pasted item is visible.

4 The selection is added on a new layer

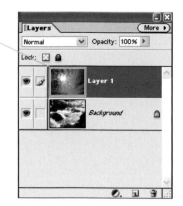

Changing the stacking order of layers can have a dramatic effect on an image that consists of two, or more, blended layers. To do this, drag the layers above, or below, one another in the Layers palette.

5 Select the new layer in the Layers palette and click here to select a merge option. This determines how the layer interacts with the one below it

6 The new layer is now merged with the one below

7 Make a selection from another image and paste it into the collage

Layered images can create much larger file sizes than single ones.

8 Select another merge option in the Layers palette. If the content in the topmost layer covers content on layers below it, the merge option will effect all of these layers

9 The final image is created once all of the layers have been added and merged

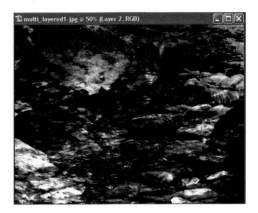

Building a skyscraper

You do not have to be an architect in order to design your own skyscraper. Just by changing the perspective of a building you can create the impression that it is towering up into the sky. To do this:

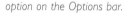 Capture an image of a building and make a selection as required

 In Paint Shop Pro, use the Deform tool in the Tools toolbar and select the Perspective Correction tool option.

 In PhotoImpact, use the Transform tool in the Tool panel and use the Perspective option on the Options bar.

2 Select Image>Transform>Perspective from the Menu bar

 Once the skyscraper has been completed, clone the background to fill in the hole that appears as a result of the change in perspective.

3 Drag here to change the perspective of the building

Pushing over a building

With a combination of trick proportions and some carefully staged images, it is possible to create a superhero-type image of someone attempting to push over a building or monument. To do this:

1 Capture an image of the building or monument that is going to be pushed over

2 Capture an image of someone pushing against an object

In Paint Shop Pro, use the Freehand Selection tool.

In PhotoImpact, use the Lasso tool.

3 Select the Polygonal Lasso tool and select the person pushing. Select Edit>Copy from the Menu bar

In Paint Shop Pro, select Edit> Paste>Paste as New Layer from the Menu bar.

In PhotoImpact, select Edit> Paste>As Object from the Menu bar.

4 Select the building image and select Edit>Paste from the Menu bar to place the selection. It will be placed on a new layer

5 Select the Zoom tool and zoom in on the pasted item

6 Select the Eraser tool and drag to remove any unwanted parts around the selection

7 Select the Move tool and drag the person pushing into the required position

 In Paint Shop Pro, use the Deform tool in the Tools toolbar.

 Make color adjustments as required to the two images so that they are as similar as possible.

8 Select Image>Transform>Free Transform from the Menu bar

 In PhotoImpact, use the Transform tool in the Tool panel.

9 Drag here to resize the person pushing the building

Creating an apparition

Some famous forged photographs of the past have included ghostly figures that give images a supernatural effect. With digital images a similar effect can be achieved by combining two images and making one of them into an apparition. To do this:

Capture an image that you want to use as the apparition. If necessary, stage the image to enhance the effect

Select the Polygonal Lasso tool and select the apparition figure. Select Edit>Copy from the Menu bar

In Paint Shop Pro, select Edit> Paste>Paste as New Layer from the Menu bar.

Select the main image and select Edit>Paste from the Menu bar to place the selection. It will be placed on a new layer

In PhotoImpact, use the Lasso tool and select Edit>Paste>As Object from the Menu bar.

4 Select the Zoom
tool and zoom in
on the pasted item

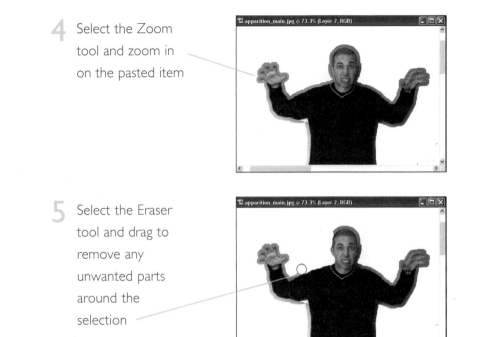

5 Select the Eraser
tool and drag to
remove any
unwanted parts
around the
selection

 In Paint Shop Pro, use the Deform tool in the Tools toolbar.

6 Select Image>Transform>Free Transform from the Menu bar

7 Drag here to resize the apparition figure

 In PhotoImpact, use the Transform tool in the Tool panel.

In Paint Shop Pro, select Layers> Properties from the Menu bar to access the Opacity settings.

In PhotoImpact, the transparency level can be set in the Layer Manager.

Apply filter effects to the apparition figure once opacity has been applied to further enhance the ghostly effect.

8 Access the Layers palette and click on the apparition figure layer to select it. Drag here to reduce the opacity of the figure (this makes it semi-transparent)

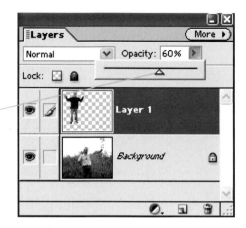

9 Once the opacity has been reduced the figure takes on a ghostly appearance

Giving your images the edge

By adding filter effects images can be made to stand out by emphasizing their edges. To do this:

1 Open an image

2 Access the Filters palette and double click on the Poster Edges filter

In Paint Shop Pro, select Effects> Edge Effects from the Menu bar.

In PhotoImpact, select Effect> Emphasize Edges from the Menu bar.

3 Make the required selections and click OK

4 The effect is applied to the image or a selection within it

Creating an animation

If you are producing images for use on the Web or for emailing to family and friends, an extra dimension can be added to them by creating animations. This consists of a series of images that are placed on separate layers and then played in sequence to create an animated effect. This has to be done with images in the GIF file format rather than the JPEG file format, which is more commonly used for photographic images. To create an animation:

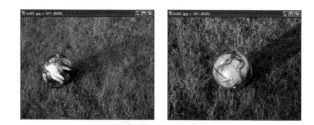

Animated images are created in the GIF file format.

1 Capture a sequence of images that will be effective when combined in an animation

Animated GIF images can be displayed on a website. However, make sure the file size is not too large, otherwise it may take a long time to download.

2 For each image, select File>Save As from the Menu bar

3 Click here and select Compuserve GIF as the file format

4 Click Save to save each image as a GIF

5 In the Index Color box, enter 256 as the number of colors and Forced as None. Click OK

6 In the GIF Options box, check on Normal

In PhotoImpact, various animated effects can be created by selecting Effect>Creative>Animation Studio from the Menu bar.

7 Select File>New from the Menu bar to open a new, blank, file

8 Select either the whole of each of the GIF images, or part of them, and select Edit>Copy from the Menu bar

9 Select the background layer in the blank file and select Edit>Paste from the Menu bar. The selection is placed in the new image

10 Copy and paste the rest of the images so that they are all on individual layers within the image

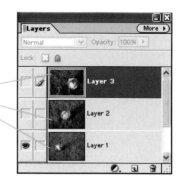

11 Select File>Save for Web from the Menu bar

12 Check on the Animate box

Animations that play continuously can quickly become tiring for the person who is viewing them.

13 Check on the Loop box if you want the animation to play continuously

14 Click OK

15 In the Save Optimized As box, give the animation an identifiable name and click Save. The file can now be published on a website or emailed to someone who can view the animation through a browser

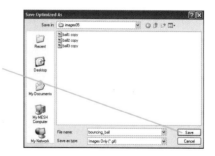

Family projects

Digital photo projects can provide hours of entertainment and education for all family members. This chapter covers some fun projects that can be undertaken with images of family members, young and old. These include changing facial features, swapping hairstyles, enhancing portraits and creating an online photo album.

Covers

Chapter Six

Facial makeovers

A popular use for digital images is changing facial features. There are a number of ways in which this can be achieved.

Cloning features

If you want to know how you would look with the features of another member of your family this can be done by cloning their features onto an image of yourself. To do this:

1. Open images of two family members. Try and ensure that they are taken in the same lighting conditions and from the same distance

The best way to ensure consistency between two images is to ask the subject to sit or stand at the same point and use a tripod to keep the camera in the same position.

This is an interesting project for seeing which features between siblings are similar.

2. Select the image on which you want to perform the makeover

3. Access the Layers palette and click here to add a new layer

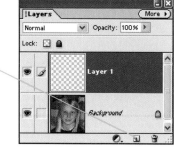

4 Select the Clone tool

In Paint Shop Pro, hold down Shift and right click to load the Clone tool.

5 Hold down Alt and click on the image from which you want to copy

In PhotoImpact, use the Clone-Paintbrush tool and hold down the Shift key and left click to load it.

6 Select the main image and drag to clone from the second image. (Make sure it is on the layer above the main image)

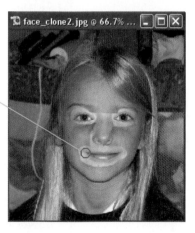

The reason the cloned selection is placed on a new layer is so that it can be edited independently from the background image.

7 Make sure the layer containing the cloned area is still selected in the Layers palette

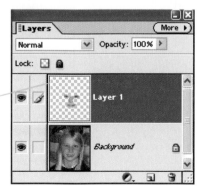

In Paint Shop Pro, use the Deform tool in the Tools toolbar.

In PhotoImpact, use the Transform tool in the Tool panel.

8 Select Image>Transform>Free Transform from the Menu bar

9 Click on the cloned area and drag here to resize the area so that it is in proportion with the main image

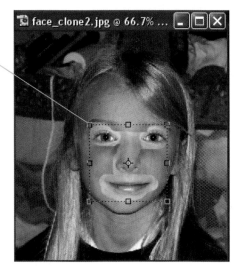

10 Select Enhance>Adjust Brightness/Contrast>Levels from the Menu bar

In Paint Shop Pro, select Adjust> Brightness and Contrast>Levels from the

Menu bar.

In PhotoImpact, select Format> Level from the Menu bar.

11 Drag these sliders to adjust the color of the cloned area so that it matches the main image as closely as possible. Click OK

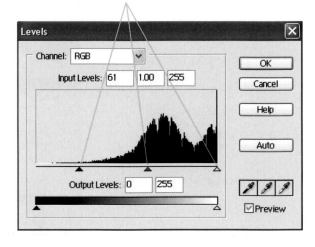

In Paint Shop Pro, select Adjust>Brightness and Contrast>Brightness/Contrast from the Menu bar.

In PhotoImpact, select Format>Brightness & Contrast from the Menu bar.

12 Select Enhance>Adjust Brightness/Contrast>Brightness/Contrast from the Menu bar

13 Drag these sliders to further adjust the color of the cloned area. Click OK

Brightness/Contrast

Brightness:	-19	OK
Contrast:	-17	Cancel
		Help
		☑ Preview

14 The final image displays the combined facial features. If required, this can be done with two or more different features from different people

face_clone2.jpg @ 100% (Layer 1, RGB)

Adding clip art

Facial makeovers can also be achieved through the use of clip art images. These can be obtained from collections on CDs (sometimes as cover discs on computer magazines) or from the Web. Once you have a clip art collection you can select the relevant facial items and add them to a photographic image. If you are using several graphical images, it is a good idea to store them in a single image file, with each graphic on a different layer. This will then enable you to access the file and copy and paste the relevant items. To do this:

1 Open a clip art image in your image editing program

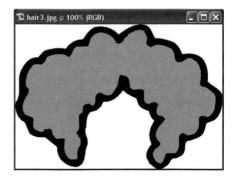

2 Select the Polygonal Lasso tool or the Magic Wand tool and make a selection

In Paint Shop Pro, use the Freehand Selection tool.

In PhotoImpact, use the Lasso tool.

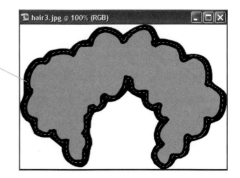

3 Select Edit>Copy from the Menu bar

4 Select File>New from the Menu bar, to open a new file in which you can save the clip art elements

5 By default, the
dimensions of the
new image will be
the same as the
selection that has
been copied

6 Since the new image
will store more than
one item, increase
the size of the new
image accordingly
and click OK

7 Click here in the
Layers palette to
create a new layer

*In Paint Shop Pro,
select Edit>
Paste>Paste as
New Layer from
the Menu bar.*

8 Select Edit>Paste
to paste the
selection onto a
new layer in the
new image

*In PhotoImpact,
select Edit>
Paste>As Object
from the Menu
bar.*

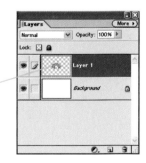

9 Copy and paste
   as many clip art
   items as required.
   Each one will be
   placed on a new
   layer

10 Select File>Save As from
    the Menu bar to save the
    file. Save the file in the
    program's proprietary file
    format. Make sure the
    Layers box is checked on.
    This will retain all of the
    layer information in the
    file and allow each item to
    be used independently

*A proprietary file
format is one
that is unique to
the program in
which the file is
created. Proprietary formats
usually allow more levels of
information to be stored. Once
an image has been saved in a
proprietary format, copies can
then be made in more common
formats such as JPEG.*

11 Open the image into
    which you want to
    copy the clip art items

12 Resize the two files so they are both visible

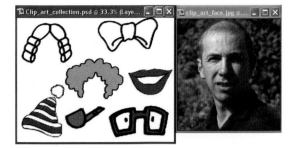

13 Click on a clip art item and drag it onto the other image

In Paint Shop Pro, use the Deform tool in the Tools toolbar.

In PhotoImpact, use the Transform tool in the Tool panel.

14 Drag the clip art item into position with the Move tool and drag here to resize it as required

15 Click and drag here to rotate a clip art item as required

When clip art items are added to the background image they are all placed on new layers. This means they can be moved and edited independently.

16 Add more clip art items to further enhance the comic effect of the image

Change the stacking order of layers in the Layers palette to ensure each element appears in the right order. To do this, drag the layers up or down in the Layers palette.

Distortion special effects

Distorting facial features is always a popular project when dealing with family and friends. This can be done with a variety of filters, some of which require manual manipulation, and others which apply the distortion automatically.

Liquify filter

This is a filter that enables you to apply manual distortions with a variety of effects. To do this:

In Paint Shop Pro, select Effects> Distortion Effects from the Menu bar for similar options.

In PhotoImpact, select Effect> Distort from the Menu bar for similar options.

1   Open a file containing a large image of your subject

2   Select Filter>Distort>Liquify from the Menu bar

3   Click here and drag on the image to create a Warp effect

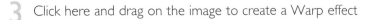

4 Click here and drag on the image to create a Turbulence (or ripple) effect

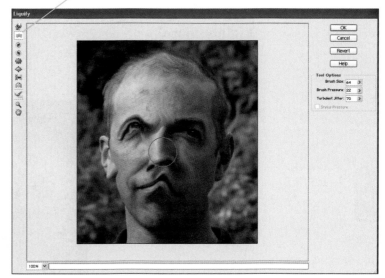

Different effects can be created by dragging across an image or clicking and holding at the same point, without moving the mouse.

5 Click here and click on the image to twirl an area clockwise or counterclockwise

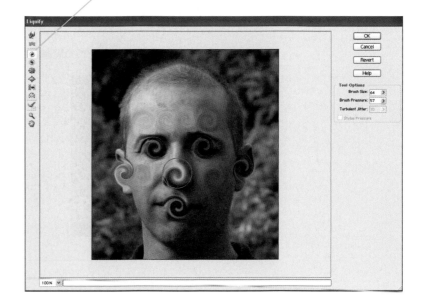

6 Click here and click on the image to create a Pucker effect

It is best not to use distortion effects on someone else's image, unless you have asked them first and let them see the results.

7 Click here and click on the image to create a Bloat effect

8 Click OK to add the distortion effects

Pinch filter

1 Select Filter>Distort>Pinch from the Menu bar

2 Drag here to specify the amount of the effect to be applied

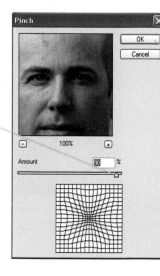

3 Click OK

In general, a little goes a long way when using distortion effects.

4 The Pinch effect is applied to the image

Spherize filter

1 Select Filter>Distort>Spherize from the Menu bar

2 Drag here to specify the amount of the effect to be applied

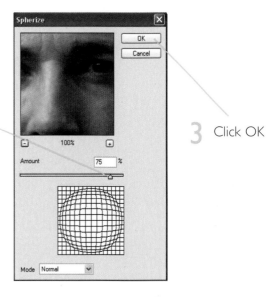

3 Click OK

4 The Spherize effect is applied to the image

Twirl filter

1 Select Filter>Distort>Twirl from the Menu bar

2 Drag here to specify the amount of the effect to be applied

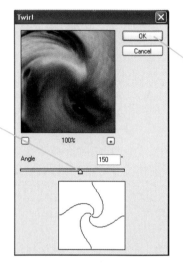

3 Click OK

4 The Twirl effect is applied to the image

Wave filter

1 Select Filter>Distort>Wave from the Menu bar

2 Drag these sliders to specify the amount of the effect to be applied

The Wave filter can be effectively used on images of water, or selections of water within an image.

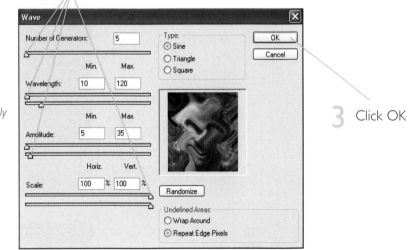

3 Click OK

4 The Wave effect is applied to the image

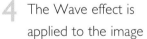

Swapping hairstyles

People sometimes imagine what they would look like if they had a different hairstyle. In the digital world it is possible to achieve this and it can be fun to see how different people look with each other's hair. To do this:

1 Open an image of the person whose hair you want to copy

In Paint Shop Pro, use the Freehand Selection tool.

2 Select the Polygonal Lasso tool and make a selection of the hair

In PhotoImpact, use the Lasso tool.

3 Select Edit>Copy from the Menu bar

4 Open the second image and select Edit>Paste from the Menu bar to add the hair

In Paint Shop Pro, select Edit> Paste>Paste as New Layer from the Menu bar and then use the Deform tool in the Tools toolbar.

In PhotoImpact, select Edit> Paste>As Object from the Menu bar and then use the Transform tool in the Tool panel.

5 Select the Move tool and drag here to resize the hair as required

6 Drag here to move the hair into position

7 In the Layers palette make sure the hair layer is still selected

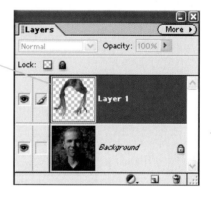

8 Use the Brightness/ Contrast command and the Levels command to match the color of the hair with that of the main image

Softening family portraits

An effective technique for giving family portraits a more professional appearance is to soften and blur the border around the portrait. To do this:

1   Open an image of a family member or a family group

HOT TIP

When making the selection, make sure that there is enough space between the selection and the outer border of the image. This will enable the feather effect to be applied properly.

2   Select either the Elliptical Marquee tool or the Rectangular Marquee tool

3   Drag to make a selection around the main subject

In Paint Shop Pro, select Selections> Modify>Feather and then Selections>Invert from the Menu bar.

In PhotoImpact, select Selection> Soften and then Selection>Invert from the Menu bar.

4 Choose Select>Feather from the Menu bar

5 Enter a Feather value (this is the number of pixels around the radius of the selection that will be blurred)

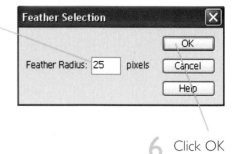

6 Click OK

7 Choose Select>Inverse from the Menu bar to select the background of the image

The background of the image is taken from the currently selected background color in color palette in the Toolbox.

8 Delete the background (Backspace key or Delete key) and crop the final image as required

Creating a family Web photo album

With the increasing ubiquity of the World Wide Web, more and more people are now looking to create an online presence. One of the ways to do this is to create a Web photo album that can be viewed online by family and friends. Once this has been created the files will have to be published on the Web. This can be done with one of the free online Web publishing services such as Yahoo Geocities (http://geocities.yahoo.com) or AOL (www.aol.com). Alternatively you could register your own domain name and find a Web hosting service for your pages. This offers more flexibility but there is usually a fee for a Web hosting service. Before a Web photo album is published it has to be created:

Paint Shop Pro and PhotoImpact do not have an option for creating Web photo albums.

In PhotoImpact, use the Web commands on the Menu bar for various Web publishing options.

1 Select File>Create Web Photo Gallery from the Menu bar

2 Click here to select a style for the Web Photo Gallery

3 Enter an email address for the Gallery

4 Select source and destination folders

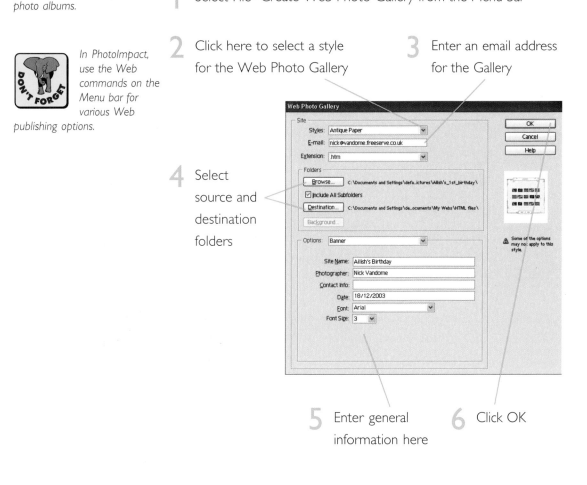

5 Enter general information here

6 Click OK

7 The Photo Gallery will be created and displayed in your browser

Keep image file sizes as small as possible if they are going to be displayed as Web pages.

8 Click on a thumbnail to display the larger version of an image

9 Click here to move through the images in the Photo Gallery

Interior design projects

Redecorating a room is often an expensive and stressful process. Questions about paint color, wallpaper and carpets are numerous and there is always a bit of apprehension about how the final job is going to look. However, the projects in this chapter show how digital images can come to the rescue of the nervous interior designer and avert many potential home improvement disasters.

Covers

Chapter Seven

Creating a panorama of a room

Digital photography and image editing offers some great possibilities when it comes to interior design and redecorating your home. Instead of having to guess how a particular paint color or wallpaper will look in your home, it is possible to create a reasonable impression of how your redecorating might look, before you have even picked up a paint brush or hung the first roll of wallpaper. Before you start experimenting, it can be useful to create a panorama of the room that is going to be decorated. To do this:

In Paint Shop Pro, panoramas have to be created manually by adding each image to a different layer so that they overlap at the edges and then altering the opacity so that the images below blend into the ones above them.

In PhotoImpact, select Edit>Stitch from the Menu bar to create a panorama effect.

1 Capture images of the room. Make sure that each image is captured from the same point and that they overlap each other by at least 20%

2 Select File>Create Photomerge from the Menu bar

3 Click Browse to locate the images you want to use

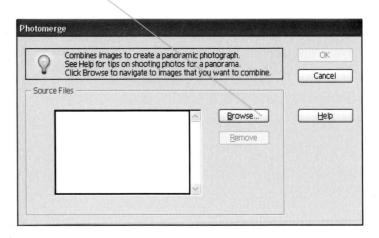

4 Select the files and click Open

Some digital cameras have a facility for creating panoramas within the camera itself.

5 In the Photomerge dialog box the source files are displayed. Click OK to create the room panorama

6 The panorama is created automatically and displayed in the Photomerge dialog box. Click OK to create the final image

Sometimes, if images are not a perfect match they have to be added manually by dragging them into the Photomerge image.

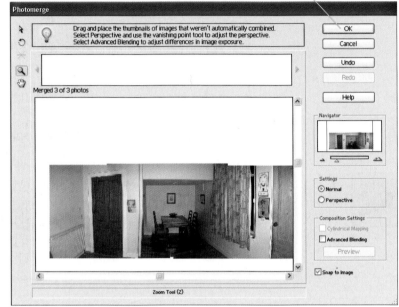

7 Select the Crop tool and drag to remove any uneven edges around the image

A panorama of a room may not be completely accurate and there may be some distortion between the images. However, it is a good way to create an overview of how a room looks.

Repainting a room

Before you physically start repainting a room it is possible to create the type of effect that will be achieved with a particular color. Although the digital effect will not be identical to the real one, it can be very effective for an artist's impression of how the room could look. To do this:

The color can also be created by changing the hue and saturation of the selection. This preserves more of the shading of the selection.

In Paint Shop Pro, use the Paint Brush tool.

1 Open an image of a room and make a selection with the Polygonal Marquee tool or the Magic Wand tool

2 Select the Pencil tool and a suitable pencil thickness

3 Drag over the selection to apply the color that is currently selected in the foreground color box in the Toolbox

4 Make another selection and apply a color with the Pencil tool. If you are painting another wall, make the color slightly lighter or darker from the initial one, to take into account lighting and shading effects

Once a solid color has been added to an image it can easily be selected with the Magic Wand tool and changed, if required.

5 Repaint the rest of the walls and any other areas such as the baseboards (also called skirting boards) to create the final effect

Mixing your own paint

As any good decorator knows, it is important to be able to experiment with different paint colors before you make your final choice. With digital image editing it is possible to do this without even having to open a single pot of paint:

1 Open an image
   on which you
   want to apply
   your test colors

*In Paint Shop Pro,
use the Materials
palette to select
and edit colors.
This can be
accessed by selecting View>
Palettes>Materials from the
Menu bar.*

2 Click here on the
   Toolbox

3 Drag
   here to
   select a
   base
   color

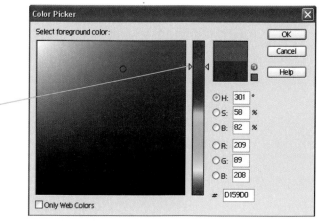

4 Enter values here to specify the hue, saturation and brightness of a color

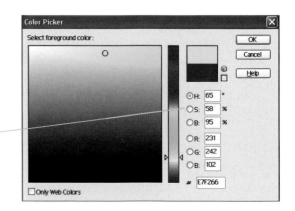

5 Enter values here to specify the red, green and blue values of a color

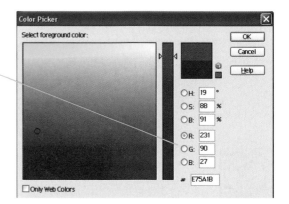

Hexadecimal colors are ones created using six digits or letters. This color format is most commonly used for colors that are going to be displayed on the Web.

6 Enter values here to specify a hexadecimal color

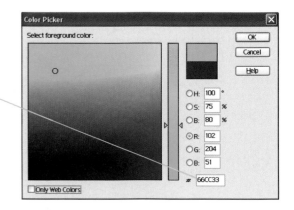

7 The final color is shown here

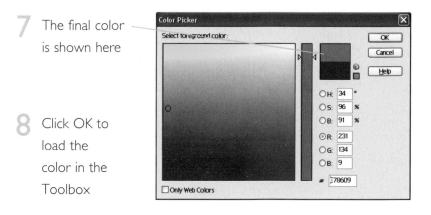

8 Click OK to load the color in the Toolbox

9 Select the Pencil tool and drag on an image to apply the color. Several colors can be placed side by side, in the same way as using "tester" paint pots on a real wall

Wallpapering

As with repainting, it is possible to create a digital impression of how a room would look with new wallpaper. To do this:

1 Capture an image of the wallpaper you want to use

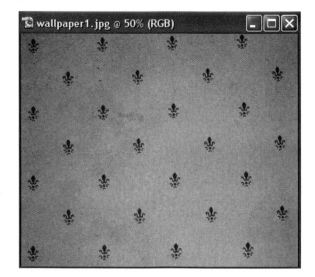

In Paint Shop Pro, select Image> Resize from the Menu bar.

2 To create realistic proportions, resize the wallpaper image by selecting Image>Resize>Image Size from the Menu bar

3 Enter a reasonably small value here (and make sure the Resample Image box is checked on)

In PhotoImpact, select Format> Image Size from the Menu bar.

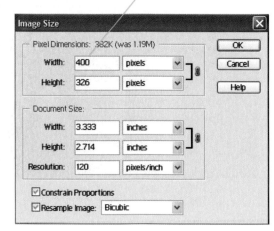

4 Open the wallpaper image and the image of the room next to each other

In PhotoImpact, use the Clone-Paintbrush tool.

5 Select the Clone tool. Hold down Alt and click on the wallpaper image to load the Clone tool

6 Drag on the room image to clone the wallpaper image onto the walls

Hanging curtains

When dealing with fabric material items, such as curtains, a slightly different technique is required to change them, compared with solid surfaces such as walls. To do this:

1 Capture an image containing the curtains you want to change and make an appropriate selection

In Paint Shop Pro, click on the Pattern tab in the Materials palette.

In PhotoImpact, use the Texture button on the Attributes toolbar.

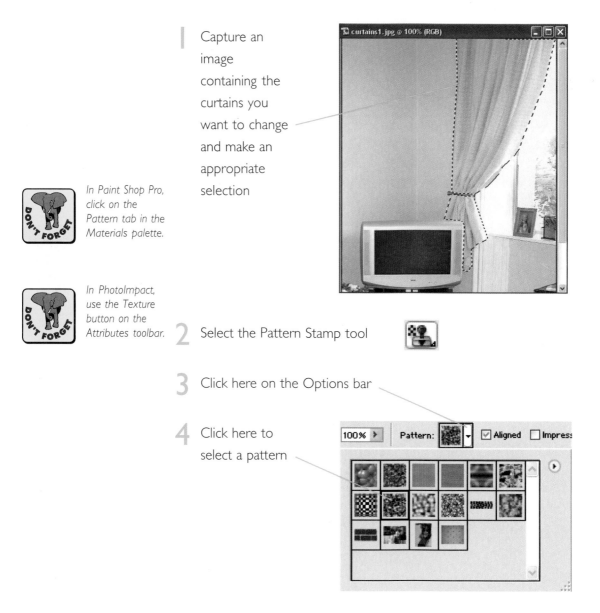

2 Select the Pattern Stamp tool

3 Click here on the Options bar

4 Click here to select a pattern

5 Click here on the Options bar to access the Opacity option

The greater the opacity the less transparent an image, or effect, is and vice versa.

6 Drag this slider to set the Opacity level

7 Drag over the curtains to apply the pattern. Because the opacity setting ensures the pattern is partially transparent, the texture of the curtain is still visible through the pattern

New patterns can be created by opening an image, or making a selection in an image, and selecting Edit> Define Pattern from the Menu bar.

Laying a new carpet

If you want to see how a new carpet would look in a room, this effect can be achieved by changing the hue of the existing one. This will create a new color, while retaining the texture of the current carpet. To do this:

1 Open an image containing the carpet and, with the Polygonal Lasso tool, make an asymmetrical selection of the carpet area

In Paint Shop Pro, use the Freehand Selection tool and select Adjust> Hue and Saturation>Hue/Saturation/ Lightness from the Menu bar.

In PhotoImpact, use the Lasso tool and select Format>Hue & Saturation from the Menu bar.

2 Select Enhance>Adjust Color>Hue/Saturation from the Menu bar

3 Check on the Colorize box and create a new effect by dragging the sliders

4 The color of the carpet is changed, but the original tone remains the same

Laying a wooden floor

One of the problems about laying a wooden floor in the digital world, as with the real one, is the fact that there are usually numerous obstacles in the way. Digitally, this can be overcome by placing the furniture and similar items on a different layer and then placing the wooden floor below them. To do this:

1 Capture an image to which you want to add a wooden floor

Samples of wooden flooring can usually be found in hardware and home improvement stores.

2 Capture an image of a wooden floor. Try and capture it at the same distance and angle as the room image

3 Select the Magic Wand tool and click on an area of the carpet in the main image to select it

...cont'd

4 With the first area
still selected hold
down Shift and click
on other areas to
select them

*In Paint Shop Pro,
select Selections>
Invert from the
Menu bar.*

5 Choose Select>Inverse from the Menu bar

6 Select Edit>Copy from the Menu bar

*In PhotoImpact,
select Selection>
Invert from the
Menu bar.*

7 Access the Layers
palette and click here
to create a new layer

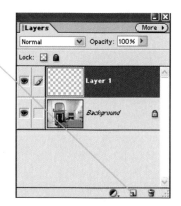

*In Paint Shop Pro,
select Edit>
Paste>Paste as
New Layer from
the Menu bar.*

8 With the new layer
selected, select
Edit>Paste from the
Menu bar

*In PhotoImpact,
select Edit>
Paste>As Object
from the Menu
bar.*

9 The selection should
be pasted in exactly
the same position as
the background

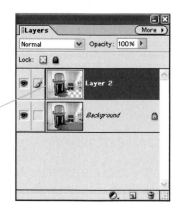

10 Select the floor image, make a selection with the Rectangular Marquee tool and select Edit>Copy from the Menu bar

11 Select the room image and select the background layer in the Layers palette

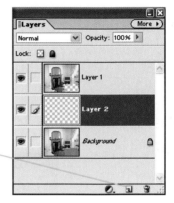

12 Click here on the Layers palette to add a new layer

In Paint Shop Pro, select Edit> Paste>Paste as New Layer from the Menu bar.

13 Select Edit>Paste from the Menu bar to add the selection of the wooden floor

In PhotoImpact, select Edit> Paste>As Object from the Menu bar.

14 Click here to hide
the top layer

In Paint Shop Pro, use the Deform tool in the Tools toolbar to resize the floor image.

In PhotoImpact, use the Transform tool on the Tool panel.

15 Select the Move
tool and click and
drag to resize the
floor image

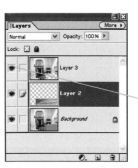

16 Click here to reveal
the top layer again

17 The wooden floor
should appear
underneath the
furniture

Changing the furniture

Instead of redecorating a room, it is also possible to redesign it by adding different furniture into the existing decor. To do this:

In Paint Shop Pro, use the Freehand Selection tool.

In PhotoImpact, use the Lasso tool.

1 Open an image and, with the Polygonal Lasso tool, select the furniture you want to remove

2 Press Delete or Backspace to remove the selection

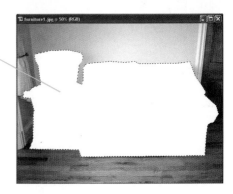

3 Open an image containing the new furniture and select an item using the Polygonal Lasso tool

4 Select the Edit>Copy from the Menu bar

In Paint Shop Pro, select Edit> Paste>Paste as New Layer from the Menu bar.

In PhotoImpact, select Edit> Paste>As Object from the Menu bar.

5 Select the first image and select Edit>Paste from the Menu bar

6 Repeat Steps 3–5 for all of the items you want to include. Each item is placed on a separate layer

7 To make the furniture the correct proportions for the room, select an item with the Move tool

In Paint Shop Pro, use the Deform tool in the Tools toolbar.

8 Select the Move tool and click and drag here to resize the item

In PhotoImpact, use the Transform tool on the Tool panel.

9 Resize all of
the furniture
items and drag
them into
position with
the Move tool

10 Access the Layers
palette and hide all of
the furniture items by
clicking here to hide
the eye icons

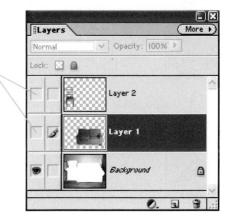

11 The furniture
items are
hidden,
although they
are still
contained in
the image

12 Select the
background
image in the
Layers palette

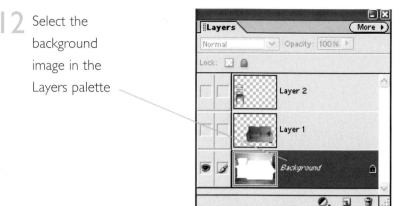

In PhotoImpact,
use the Clone-
Paintbrush tool.

13 Select the
Clone tool
and clone
the area not
covered by
the furniture

Numerous pieces
of furniture can
be used within a
single image. Use
the Layers palette
to hide and reveal the different
items as required. This means
that several combinations can be
tried with the same background.

14 Display all
of the
layers in
the Layers
palette to
reveal the
final image

To display a
hidden layer,
click on the box
that contained the
eye icon, to
reveal it again.

Lighting projects

Through the creative use of lighting, digital images can be transformed to appear as if they have been captured with professional lighting equipment. This chapter shows how to improve the lighting of images and add a variety of lighting special effects.

Covers

Chapter Eight

Throwing some light on the subject

Even though sunlight is one of the best conditions for capturing images, it can cause some problems. One of these occurs when an image is captured with the sun directly behind the main subject. This makes the subject shaded and creates a dull impression in what is otherwise a bright image. However, this can be rectified with a project that throws light on the main subject. To do this:

1 Open an image where the main subject is shaded against a bright background

In Paint Shop Pro, use the Freehand Selection tool and then apply brightness and contrast color correction to the image.

2 Select the Polygonal Lasso tool and select the main subject

...cont'd

In PhotoImpact, make a selection with the Lasso tool and select Effect> Photographic>Enhance Lighting from the Menu bar.

3 Select Enhance>Adjust Lighting>Fill Flash from the Menu bar

4 Drag this slider to change the brightness of the selection

6 Click OK

Adjust Fill Flash

Lighter: 55

OK
Cancel
Help

☑ Preview

Saturation: +10

5 Drag this slider to change the saturation of the selection

7 The main subject should now match the background in terms of brightness and saturation

fill_flash_initial.jpg @ 66.7% (RGB)

No more washed-out backgrounds

Even with the most sophisticated camera, images can suffer from areas of overexposure. This is where one area of the image is brighter than the rest and occurs most frequently when there is a light background and a duller foreground. This can be corrected by applying a reverse technique to that for brightening a shaded main subject. To do this:

1 Open an image where the background is brighter than the foreground and looks "washed-out" in comparison

In Paint Shop Pro, use the Freehand Selection tool and then apply brightness and contrast color correction to the image.

In PhotoImpact, use the Lasso tool and then apply brightness and contrast color correction to the image.

2 Select the Polygonal Lasso tool or the Magic Wand tool and select the background

3 Select Enhance>Adjust Lighting>Adjust Backlighting from the Menu bar

4 Drag this slider to change the brightness of the selection

5 Click OK

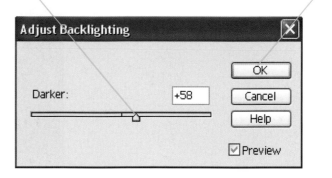

6 The background should now match the background in terms of brightness

 In Paint Shop Pro, select Adjust> Sharpness> Sharpen from the Menu bar.

 In PhotoImpact, select Effect> Sharpen>Sharpen from the Menu bar.

7 Sometimes backgrounds can appear slightly fuzzy and out of focus. If this is the case, select the background and select Filter> Sharpen>Sharpen from the Menu bar to improve the focus

Under the spotlight

A variety of lighting effects can be achieved with expensive photographic lighting equipment. However, similar effects can be achieved through a variety of lighting projects. These include using a spotlight effect to highlight an area of an image. To do this:

1 Open an image containing the subject you want to highlight

 In Paint Shop Pro, lighting effects can be added by selecting Effects> Illumination Effects>Lights from the Menu bar.

2 Select Filter>Render>Lighting Effects from the Menu bar

3 Click here and select the Spotlight option

 In PhotoImpact, lighting effects can be added by selecting Effect> Illumination from the Menu bar.

4 Drag here to change the position of the spotlight

5 Change these settings to edit the spotlight effect

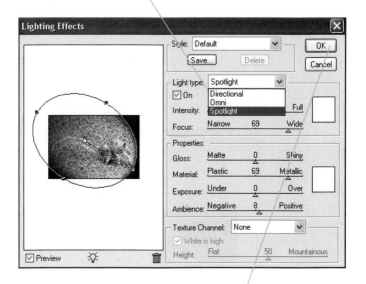

6 Click OK to apply the spotlight effect

7 The spotlight effect is added to the original image

More lighting special effects

The Lighting Effects dialog box also contains a variety of lighting special effects that can be applied to an image. To access these:

1 Select Filter>Render>Lighting Effects from the Menu bar

2 Click here and select a lighting effect

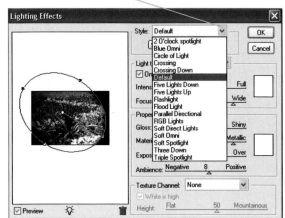

The amount and intensity of a lighting effect can be altered by dragging on the resizing markers on the image in the Lighting Effects dialog box.

3 Edit the lighting effect by changing any of the settings in the dialog box. Click OK to apply the effect

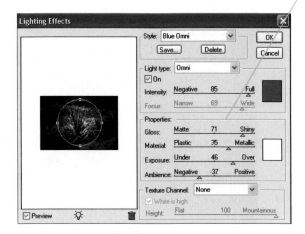

Blue Omni

Circle of Light

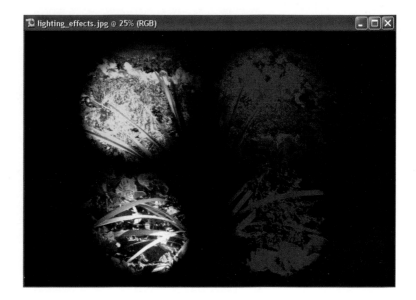

Five Lights Down

 With multiple lighting effects within an image, each element can be edited independently from the others.

Flashlight

RGB Light

Triple Spotlight

Adding some flare

Lens flare is the bright glare that can occur in images that are captured pointing directly into sunlight. In most cases it is best to avoid this, but sometimes it can create an interesting effect when added to an image. To do this:

1 Open an image to which you want to add lens flare (it is most effective if the image is fairly brightly lit)

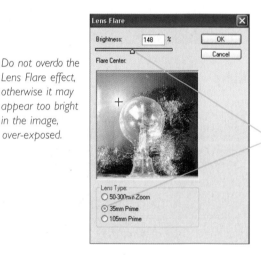

Do not overdo the Lens Flare effect, otherwise it may appear too bright in the image, making it look over-exposed.

2 Select Filter>Render>Lens Flare from the Menu bar

3 Apply settings for the lens flare effect and click OK

4 The lens flare effect is added to the image

Creating a halo

We all like to think of ourselves a bit angelic from time to time and this project allows you to enhance the impression by adding a halo over someone's head.

1 Open an image to which you want to add a halo

2 Access the Layers palette and click here to add a new layer

In Paint Shop Pro, use the Ellipse Selection tool.

3 Select the Elliptical Marquee tool and make an elliptical selection on the new layer

In Paint Shop Pro, use the Flood Fill tool and the Smudge tool.

In PhotoImpact, use the Bucket Fill tool or one of the brush tools.

4 Select the Paint Bucket tool and fill the selection with white

5 Select the Elliptical Marquee tool again and make a smaller selection, inside the existing one

6 Delete the selection

Reduce the opacity level of the halo layer in the Layers palette to give it a more subtle effect.

7 Select the Blur tool and drag around the edges of the halo to complete the effect

Artistic projects

Digital photography is not exclusive to people who want to create photo-realistic images. For anyone with an artistic talent there are a variety of techniques and projects that can be used to create digital works of art. These include numerous painting techniques, creating sculptures and adding the impression of speed and reflections to images.

Covers

Chapter Nine

Becoming an impressionist painter

By using digital imaging software even the most unartistic people can turn their images into works of art. One option is to achieve an impressionist effect by making images look as though they have been created by painting individual colored dots on a canvas, rather than long brush strokes. This can be achieved through the use of image editing tools or through the use of special effect filters.

Using tools

In Paint Shop Pro, artistic effects can be created by selecting Effects>Art Media Effects or Artistic Effects from the Menu bar.

In PhotoImpact, artistic effects can be created by selecting Effect>Artistic from the Menu bar.

1 Capture an image that will be effective for turning into an impressionist painting

2 Select the Impressionist Brush tool and make suitable selections in the Options bar

3 Drag over the image to create the impressionist effect

Using filters

1 Capture an image
that will be effective
for turning into an
impressionist painting

*The Effects
palette can
also be used
to change the
appearance of
an image, but this just applies
the effect, without any
additional dialog boxes.*

2 Open the Filters
palette and double
click on a suitable filter
(in this example, it is
the Craquelure filter)

3 Make the appropriate
selections in the dialog
box and click OK

4 The filter effect is
added to the image

Creating works of art

In addition to creating an impressionist effect, it is also possible to convert digital images into works of art in a variety of styles. This is done in the same way as with the impressionist effect, that is, selecting a filter and applying the effect to an image. The effect can be edited by changing the settings in the filter dialog box. Some artistic effects that can be achieved are:

Dry Brush

When adding artistic effects with filters, a low value setting in the filter dialog box sometimes creates the best results.

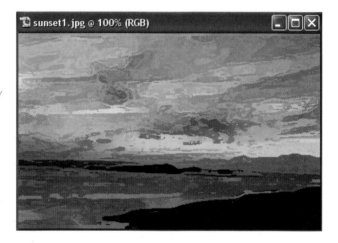

Film Grain

Paint Daubs

Some filter effects can exaggerate dark areas in an image to the point where it is too dark.

Rough Pastels

Creating a stained glass window

Real stained glass windows can look stunning, but they are expensive and intricate to make. As a cheaper and quicker alternative, windows in digital images can have a stained glass effect applied to them, either through the use of filters or manually with the use of layers.

Using filters

1   Capture an image that contains a reasonably large window area

In Paint Shop Pro and PhotoImpact, use the layers method described on pages 155–157.

2   Select the Polygonal Lasso tool or the Rectangular Marquee tool and select the window area

3   Access the Filters palette and double click on the Stained Glass filter

...cont'd

*An interesting
stained glass
effect can also
be created by
selecting a person
or an object and applying the
Stained Glass filter to this
selection.*

4 Make the required
selections in the Stained
Glass dialog box and
click OK (the border
color is the foreground
one currently selected in
the Tools panel)

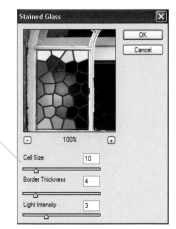

5 Select the Magic Wand
tool and click in a glass
segment to select it

6 Click here on
the Tools panel

7 Select a new
color and
click OK

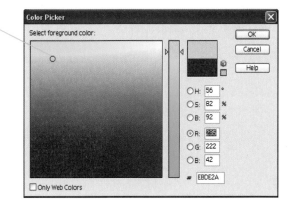

8 Select the Paint
Bucket tool and click
on the selection to
apply the new color

9 Repeat Steps 2–8
for the rest of the
segment of glass

*Each section has
to be selected
individually in
order to have
separate gradient
fills applied.*

10 If required, apply
a gradient fill to
the glass
segments, to
create a more
dramatic effect

Using layers

1 Capture an image that contains a reasonably large window area

2 Select the Zoom tool and zoom in on the window area

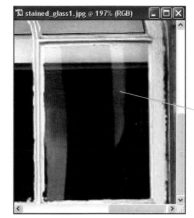

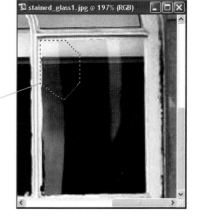

In Paint Shop Pro, use the Freehand Selection tool.

In PhotoImpact, use the Lasso tool.

3 Select the Polygonal Lasso tool and make an asymmetrical selection

4 Select Edit>Copy from the Menu bar

In Paint Shop Pro, select Edit>Paste>Paste as New Layer from the Menu bar.

In PhotoImpact, select Edit>Paste>As Object from the Menu bar.

5 Select Edit>Paste from the Menu bar

6 The selection is placed on a new layer. Position it in exactly the same place as before it was cut from the background image

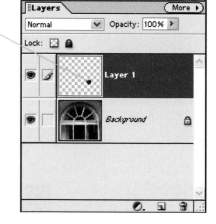

7 Select the new layer and use the Magic Wand tool to select the selection again

8 Select the Pencil tool and click here on the Toolbox

In Paint Shop Pro, use the Materials palette to select the color and use the Paint Brush tool to add the color to the selection.

9 Select a color in the Color Picker and click OK

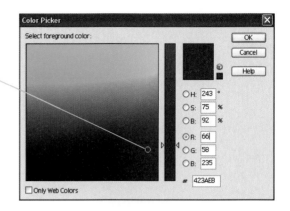

10 Drag the Pencil tool over the selection

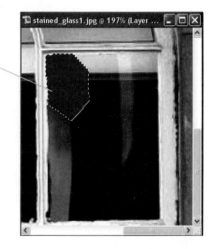

11 Repeat Steps 3–10 for the rest of the window

Creating your own sculpture

If you are more interested in creating sculptures than paintings, this can be accommodated in the digital world too. It is possible to create your own sculpture effects, or try and recreate famous sculptures. To do this:

1 Pose an image based on the sculpture you want to create

In Paint Shop Pro, use the Freehand Selection tool.

2 Select the Polygonal Lasso tool and select the required pose

In PhotoImpact, use the Lasso tool.

3 Select Edit>Copy from the Menu bar

4 Select File> New from the Menu bar

5 In the New dialog box, click OK

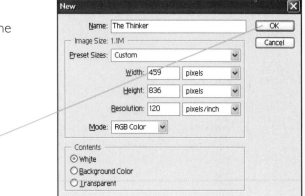

In Paint Shop Pro, select Edit> Paste>Paste as New Selection from the

Menu bar.

In PhotoImpact, select Edit> Paste>As Object from the Menu bar.

In Paint Shop Pro, select Effects> Texture Effects> Sculpture from the Menu bar and make the required selections in the dialog box.

In PhotoImpact, select Effect> Material Effect> Emboss from the Menu bar.

6 Select Edit>Paste from the Menu bar to add the selection to the new, blank, file

7 Select the image

8 Access the Filters palette and double click the Bas Relief filter

9 Make the required selections and click OK

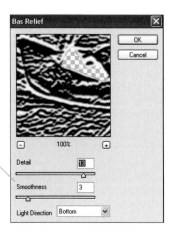

10 Select Enhance>Adjust Brightness/Contrast>Brightness/Contrast from the Menu bar

Depending on the sculpture you are trying to create, you may need to use the Eraser tool to remove certain parts of the sculpture.

11 Adjust the brightness and contrast to create the desired color for the 3D effect. Click OK

12 The final sculpture can be kept against a white background or be copied and pasted onto another, more varied, one

Framing a picture

No matter how effective images look once artistic effects have been applied, most of them will benefit from having an attractive frame placed around them. However, there is no need to go to the trouble and expense of buying and fitting a real frame. Digital frames can be applied quickly to an image and they not only provide a border but they also create an attractive 3D effect. To add a frame:

1   Open the image to which you want the frame to be applied

 In Paint Shop Pro, select Image> Picture Frame from the Menu bar.

 In PhotoImpact, select Format> Frame & Shadow from the Menu bar.

2   Access the Effects palette and double click on a frame effect (in this example it is Photo Corners)

3   The frame effect is added to the image

Brushed Aluminium frame

Ripple frame

Wood frame

Adding motion

Even though digital images are static, it is possible to create the impression of speed for either vehicles or people. This can be used in a variety of ways, to create an image of a speeding car, or someone sprinting in front of a crowd that looks blurred as the runner speeds past. To do this:

In Paint Shop Pro, use the Freehand Selection tool and select Selections>Modify>Feather from the Menu bar.

In PhotoImpact, use the Lasso tool and select Selection>Soften from the Menu bar to apply the feathering.

In Paint Shop Pro, select Adjust>Blur>Motion Blur from the Menu bar.

In PhotoImpact, select Effect>Blur>Motion Blur from the Menu bar.

1 Select the Polygonal Lasso tool

2 In the Options bar, set the Feather value to between 5–10 pixels

Feather: 10 px

3 Make a selection just outside the border of the vehicle or person

4 Select Edit>Cut from the Menu bar

5 Select Filter>Blur>Motion Blur from the Menu bar

6 Select the
required
settings for
the Motion
Blur effect
and click OK

*Make sure the
Motion Blur is
going in the same
direction as the
object.*

7 The Motion Blur settings are applied to the whole of the
remaining image

In Paint Shop Pro, select Edit>Paste>Paste as New Layer from the Menu bar.

In PhotoImpact, select Edit>Paste>As Object from the Menu bar.

8 Select Edit>Paste from the Menu bar to place the vehicle or person back in the image. The feathered edges should now merge with the blurred background

Try slightly less blurring for the wheels than the background, so that they are still identifiable.

9 For vehicles, to further enhance the effect, select the Elliptical Marquee tool and select the wheel area. Add Motion Blur as in Steps 5–6 so that the wheels appear blurred on the vehicle

Creating a reflection

When capturing images next to water, an excellent effect is to create a reflection of the main subject in the water. With effective lighting, positioning and good luck, this can be achieved when the shot is captured. However, if the natural elements are against you, it is possible to create a reflection at the image editing stage. To do this:

1 Capture an image with the main subject behind a large expanse of water

In Paint Shop Pro, use the Freehand Selection tool and select Edit> Paste>Paste as New Layer from the Menu bar.

2 With the Polygonal Lasso tool, select the main subject

In PhotoImpact, use the Lasso tool and select Edit> Paste>As Object from the Menu bar.

3 Select Edit>Copy from the Menu bar

4 Select Edit>Paste from the Menu bar

5 The selection is placed on a new layer

6 Select the selection with the Move tool and drag here to rotate it 180°

In Paint Shop Pro, use the Deform tool on the Tools toolbar to move and rotate the selection. Select Image>Mirror from the Menu bar to flip it horizontally.

In PhotoImpact, use the Transform tool on the Tool panel to move the selection and use the transform options bar to flip the selection.

When rotating the image, drag just outside the side resizing marker, rather than directly on it.

7 Select Image> Rotate> Flip Layer Horizontal from the Menu bar. This makes the selection a mirror image of the main subject

In Paint Shop Pro, use the Smudge tool and select Effects> Distortion Effects> Wave from the Menu bar.

In PhotoImpact, use the Lasso tool and select Effect>Distort> Ripple from the Menu bar.

8 Select the Blur tool and drag around the edges of the pasted item to soften them. Make sure the correct layer is selected

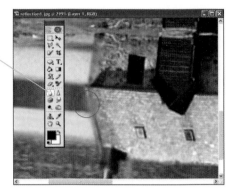

9 Select the pasted item and select Filter>Distort>Ocean Ripple from the Menu bar

10 Make the required selections and click OK

11 The pasted item has a rippled effect applied to it

In Paint Shop Pro, use the Freehand Selection tool and select Edit> Paste>Paste as New Layer from the Menu bar.

In PhotoImpact, use the Lasso tool and select Edit> Paste>As Object from the Menu bar.

12 Select the background layer and select the whole area of water with the Polygonal Lasso tool

13 Select Edit>Copy from the Menu bar

14 Select Edit>Paste from the Menu bar. The selection is placed on a new layer

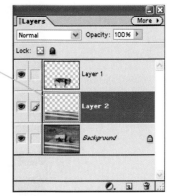

In Paint Shop Pro, select Layers> Properties to access a dialog box containing the Opacity option.

In PhotoImpact, the transparency level can be set in the Layer Manager.

15 Select the new layer and set the Opacity value to approximately 50%

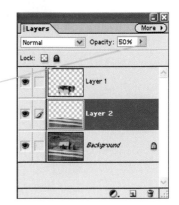

16 Drag the water layer so that it is above the layer containing the rippled object

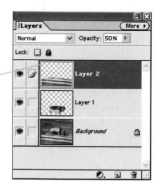

17 The final image contains the background, the rippled object and the semi-transparent layer of water

Try making the reflected object slightly longer than the one on dry land. This will give the impression of it being distorted further in the water.

18 When working on this project it can be useful to hide particular layers while working on others. To do this, click on the eye icons in the Layers palette

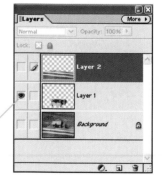

Text and images projects

Text can add an extra dimension to digital images. This chapter looks at ways in which text and images can be combined to create items that can be used in everyday life, including greetings cards, calendars and business cards.

Covers

Chapter Ten

Creating greetings cards

When working with digital images, it is possible to incorporate them into a variety of projects containing textual elements. For greetings cards this involves positioning the different elements so that they appear in the correct place once the paper has been folded to make the card. To do this:

1 Select Edit>New from the Menu bar

2 Click here to select the size of paper for the card. The size should be reasonably large, particularly if the card is going to be folded

Some image editing programs have templates for creating items such as cards and calendars. However, they do not have the overall power and versatility of programs such as Photoshop Elements, Paint Shop Pro and PhotoImpact.

3 Click OK

4 Open the image which you want to include in the card

5 Make a selection and select Edit>Copy from the Menu bar

In Paint Shop Pro, select Edit> Paste>Paste as New Selection from the Menu bar and use the Deform tool to move and resize the selection.

6 Select the blank image and select Edit>Paste from the Menu bar

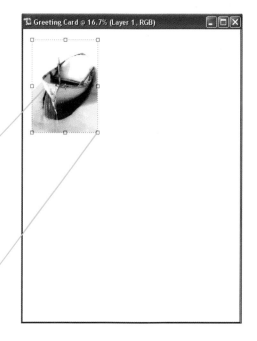

In PhotoImpact, select Edit> Paste>As Object from the Menu bar and use the Transform tool to move and resize the selection.

7 Select the Move tool and drag the image here

8 Drag here to resize the image, if required

In Paint Shop Pro, select Image>Flip from the Menu bar.

In PhotoImpact, use the selections on the Transform options bar to flip the text.

9 Select Image>Rotate>Flip Vertical from the Menu bar so that the image appears upside down

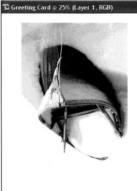

10 Select the text tool and add text as required. Drag here to rotate the text box

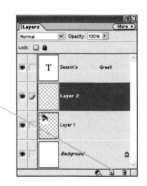

New layers are inserted above the currently selected one.

11 Click here on the Layers palette to add a new layer

12 Select the Rectangular Marquee tool and drag to make a selection on the new layer

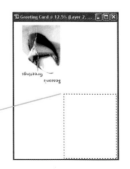

In Paint Shop Pro, use the Flood Fill tool.

In PhotoImpact, use the Bucket Fill tool.

13 Select the Paint Bucket tool and click here to create a colored background

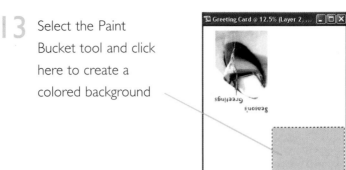

14 Select the Text tool and make any required selections in the Options bar

Once the card is completed, it can be printed and then folded as required so that the image and the inside text appear at the correct points.

15 To complete the card, click on the colored background and type the text

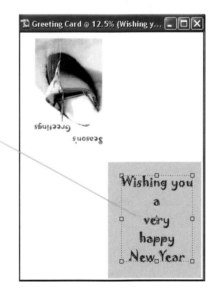

Creating calendars

More long-term projects can also be created by combining text and images. One of these is the creation of calendars, which can be produced for a variety of timescales. One way to create a calendar is to buy a pre-printed calendar list and glue this onto an image that has been printed. Another way is to create both the text and image as a single project. To do this:

1 Select Edit>New from the Menu bar

2 Click here to select the size of paper for the calendar. The size should match the overall size for the published calendar

Make sure the calendar is created at a size which can be printed on your printer.

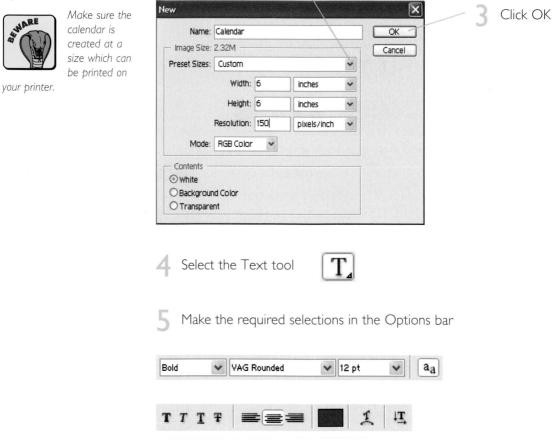

3 Click OK

4 Select the Text tool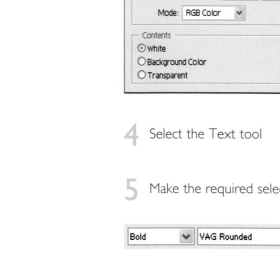

5 Make the required selections in the Options bar

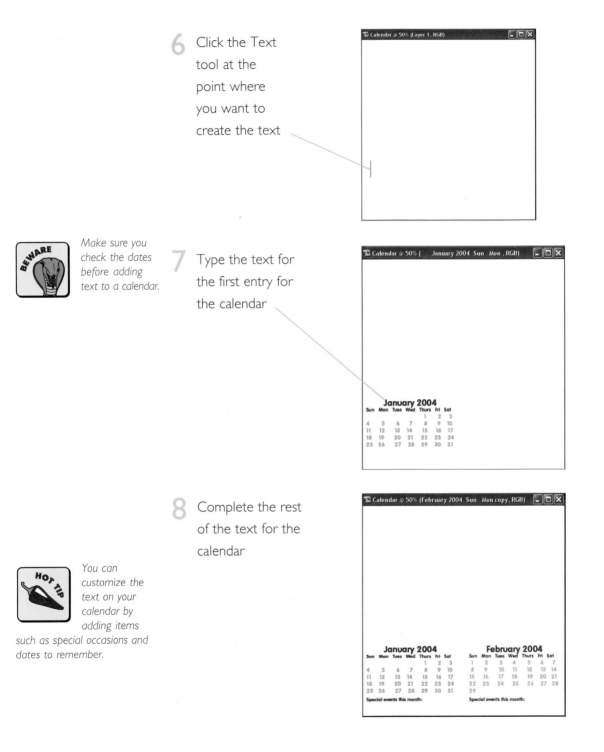

6 Click the Text
tool at the
point where
you want to
create the text

Make sure you
check the dates
before adding
text to a calendar.

7 Type the text for
the first entry for
the calendar

8 Complete the rest
of the text for the
calendar

You can
customize the
text on your
calendar by
adding items
such as special occasions and
dates to remember.

9 Open the image you want to use in the calendar. Select the area you want to use

10 Select Edit>Copy from the Menu bar

In Paint Shop Pro, select Edit> Paste>Paste as New Layer from the Menu bar.

11 Select the calendar and select Edit>Paste from the Menu bar

In PhotoImpact, select Edit> Paste>As Object from the Menu bar.

12 Select the Move tool and drag the image into position and resize it if required

13 If required, add a title to complete the calendar

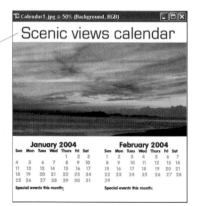

Creating business cards

Text and image projects do not have to be large scale ones. It is perfectly possible to produce something as small as business cards containing an image and the appropriate text. The biggest issues with this is the printing. If possible, print the completed cards on the thickest type of paper you can use with your printer. Even then, it may be a bit flimsy so another option is to save the completed file and use a commercial printer to print it onto thick card.

Business cards can be created either by producing multiple copies on the same page or by creating a single copy and then using the print options to print multiple copies onto a single sheet.

Multiple copies on a page

To produce multiple copies of a business card:

If you are using a commercial printer, check their requirements first, in terms of files formats and image resolution. If you are unsure about anything to do with the process, ask the printer for an explanation.

1 Select Edit>New from the Menu bar

2 Work out the dimensions for the size of your business card. Click here to select a custom size of paper for the card

3 Enter the dimensions as double the required width of the card and five times the height. Click OK

4 Access the Info palette by dragging it from the palette well

5 Select the Rectangular Marquee tool and drag on the page to create a business card-sized area

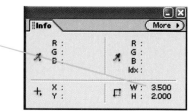

6 Use the Info palette to create the selection at half the width of the page and a fifth of the height

In Paint Shop Pro, use the Flood Fill tool.

7 Select the Paint Bucket tool and click on the selection to give it a background color. This will make it easier to see the position of the items on the page. The background color can be kept for the completed card or removed at the end

In PhotoImpact, use the Bucket Fill tool.

8 Select Edit>Cut from the Menu bar

9 Select Edit>Paste from the Menu bar to paste the selection onto a new layer. Position it above the colored box

10 Open the image you want to use in the business card. Make a selection and select Edit>Copy from the Menu bar

In Paint Shop Pro, select Edit> Paste>Paste as New Layer from the Menu bar.

11 Select the business card file and select Edit>Paste from the Menu bar

In PhotoImpact, select Edit> Paste>As Object from the Menu bar.

12 The selection is placed on a new layer in the Layers palette

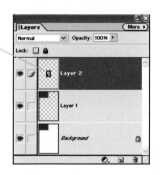

13 Select the Move tool and drag the selection into position

14 Select the Text tool and make the required selections in the Options bar

15 Click on the colored background and add text as required

If required, select the colored box and set the color to white. However, make sure the text color is still clear on the white background.

In Paint Shop Pro, select Layers> Merge>Merge All from the Menu bar.

16 Select Layer>Flatten Image from the Menu bar. This combines all of the elements of the business card into a single layer

In PhotoImpact, select Object> Merge All from the Menu bar.

17 Using the Rectangular Marquee tool, select the whole business card

In Paint Shop Pro, select Edit> Paste>Paste as New Layer from the Menu bar.

In PhotoImpact, select Edit> Paste>As Object from the Menu bar.

Before flattening the layers, save the file in the program's proprietary format to preserve the different layers.

18 Select Edit>Copy from the Menu bar

19 Select Edit>Paste from the Menu bar

20 Position the selection accordingly and repeat until the page has been filled. Each selection will be placed on a new layer

21 Select Layer>Flatten Image from the Menu bar. This combines all of the elements of the business card into a single layer

22 Save the image and print out sheets of the business card as required

Single copy

To create a single copy of a business card and then create multiple copies at the printing stage:

1   Select Edit>New from the Menu bar

2   Click here and select Custom

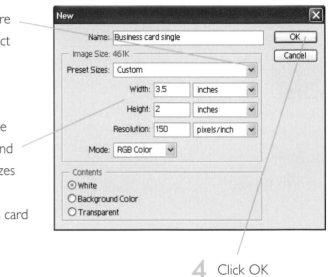

3   Enter the height and width sizes for the business card

Save a copy of the completed business card in your image editing program's proprietary file format. This will preserve the text as a separate layer and enable you to edit it at a later date, if required.

4   Click OK

5   Create the content for the business card in the same way as shown in the previous project, by adding an image and text to the file

6 Select File>Print Layouts>Print Package from the Menu bar

In Paint Shop Pro, select File>Print Layout from the Menu bar. Then select Open Template, select an appropriate template and drag the image into the required areas in the template.

7 Click here and select the appropriate number of the images required

In PhotoImpact, select File>More Print Function> Print Multiple from the Menu bar. Then select the required options in the Print Styles dialog box.

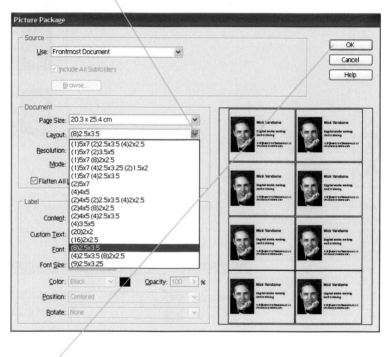

8 Click OK

9 The Picture Package
is created as a single
file, containing
multiple images

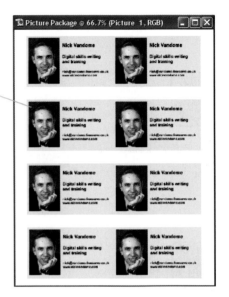

Print out your
business cards on
as thick a piece
of card as your
printer will allow.
This will make the finished article
sturdier and more professional.

10 Select File>Print Preview from the Menu bar. Check on the
Scale to Fit Media box to ensure the Picture Package file fits
onto the size of paper you are using

11 Click Print

Index

U

W

Y

Z

Downloads

Some of the images that can be downloaded to work through the projects in this book are:

animation3

blurring_the_background

calendar_image

changing_furniture2

changing_sky_color

clip_art

concocting_inedible_food

creating_a_reflection

enlarging_for_printing

film_grain

framing_a_picture

giving_images_the_edge

greeting_card_image

instant_diet

lens_flare

multi_layered1

negative

new_background1

now_you_see_them

paint_daubs

pushing_a_building1

rough_pastels

size_matters1

size_matters2

skyscraper

The full range of images can be downloaded from: www.ineasysteps.com/books/downloads or www.ineasysteps.com/books/?1840782684